Service and Support Handbook

**The Help Desk Institute
guide to Help Desk
operations and management**

Help
Desk
Institute

Editor

Jana Johnson

Assistant Editors

Julie Neider

Suzanne Katof

Help Desk Institute™

6385 Corporate Center Drive, Suite 301

Colorado Springs, Colorado 80919 USA

U.S. and Canada: 1-800-248-5667

www.thinkhdi.com

Help Desk Institute assumes no liability for error or omission.

Help Desk Institute

Table of Contents

Help Desk Institute

About the Help Desk Institute

The Help Desk Institute serves the organizations and individual professionals that provide support to users of information technology. Help Desk Institute's mission is to lead the Help Desk/Customer Support profession worldwide by setting the standards, establishing certification and training programs, and providing access to industry resources. HDI provides targeted information about the technologies, tools, and trends of the help desk and customer support industry. HDI holds the industry leading Annual Conference and Expo. HDI also offers public and on-site training, and publishes a wide range of training publications and research materials. Membership exceeds 7,500 globally with members from every continent worldwide. For more information on HDI visit **www.thinkhdi.com**.

Help Desk Institute has more that 50 local chapters operating in the US and Canada. Additional, our UK office holds numerous local networking events for our 1,000 UK members. HDI has partners in 15 additional countries to serve members.

Preface

This latest version of the Help Desk Handbook has been a collaborative effort of members from our local chapters. We asked our local chapters officers to determine the content of each of the chapters and to provide authors to write them.

This is truly a product of support professionals that face the reality of support on a day-to-day basis. You can believe what you read. These authors are leading support professionals that are telling you what you need to know. Nothing is held back. This book is real solutions provided by real support professionals. There are so many people to thank and so many contributions that I am sure I will miss some, but let me point out a few who have helped so much. Many thanks to Donna Holt and Jana Johnson for their dedication to this project and to all the individuals who contributed their time and knowledge.

At HDI we have reviewed and consolidated the input from the field. We are excited to offer this outstanding document. While we have worked to make it flow properly and to be structurally sound, one of the beauties of this book is the breadth of input. With so many authors, there are some differences in style, which we left in unless we felt it hindered the readability. We hope you enjoy, learn, and share what you learn from The Help Desk Handbook with others.

Regards,

Ron Muns, Founder Help Desk Institute

Bios

Akers, Skip
Skip Akers is currently the Webmaster (formerly Communications Officer) for the Frontier Chapter of HDI in Oklahoma City, OK. Skip is also the lead analyst for a staff of nine, highly qualified customer support professionals who maintain a 24/7/365 operation at the Federal Aviation Administration Logistics Center (FAALC). FAALC serves more than 9,000 National Airspace System customers. By benchmarking the "best of the best" in the help desk industry, Skip has been instrumental in engineering the processes and mapping automation requirements needed to develop a high level of efficiency in the FAALC's Customer Care Center.

Albright, Lynn
Lynn Albright is a manager with Blue Cross and Blue Shield of Arizona. Blue Cross and Blue Shield of Arizona is the state's largest health insurer. Lynn was a support analyst and then a lead on the help desk for more than three years. As a first line support analyst she provided call tracking, technical assistance and one-on-one training to her customers as well as training and mentoring to her peers. She has been with the company for over 7 years and was an analyst for three years. Lynn enjoys helping people and the challenge of problem solving.

Ball, Eugene
Eugene Ball, PhD is a regular speaker and writer about the customer service industry where he has 24 years of experience. With Help Desk Solutions, Inc., he has assisted companies in size from start-up to Fortune 500, government agencies and institutions of higher education in the implementation or improvement of their customer service. He is one of the founding members of the HDI's Individual Certification Standards Committee, an HDI certified instructor and an HDI certified site auditor.

Best, Diana
Diana Best has worked for the City of Tulsa for 7 years, the last four on the Telecommunications Help Desk. She has a certificate in Network Support, an Associate's Degree in Computer Information Systems - Technical Customer SupportOption, and a Bachelors of Art in Art. Diana's responsibilities include being the primary call taker for the help desk, doing software implementation & development, report design, voice mail system administration, voice talent for many of the City's automated announcements, and a variety of other small roles. She has been an HDI member for approximately one and a half years and is serving as Green Country Chapter's treasurer for the 2001/2002 year.

Bigonia, Tony
Tony Bigonia currently manages the I.S. Customer Care Center for CNH Global (Case Corporation) in Racine, Wisconsin. Prior to that he was responsible for the global Project Management of call center technology for Case's external support

desks. Before Case, Tony worked for Digital Equipment Corporation in the customer services organization for fourteen years. In Tony's spare time he holds the position as President and VP of Communications for the Professional Help Desk Association in Milwaukee, Wisconsin. Tony has a Bachelors Degree in Business Management, has a HDM certification from HDI, and recently has become a Certified Auditor for the Support Center Certification program through Help Desk Institute.

Boomershine, Jay

Jay Boomershine is a seasoned Information System Professional in the support services industry. He is currently the president for the Iowa Chapter of the Help Desk Institute (HDI). Jay has several years of experience in the help desk and customer support industry and has provided innovative, up-to-date technical solutions to several organizations locally and throughout the United States. He holds certifications from both the Help Desk Institute, Computing Technology Industry Association as well as an MIS degree from the University of Iowa's College of Business. Jay is from and currently lives in Des Moines, Iowa, where he enjoys spending time with and raising his family all while living in the "Field of Dreams".

Broome, Chris

Chris is an accomplished manager with a seventeen-year record of achievement in information systems. She has an extensive background in software evaluation, customer service and support, business process analysis and design, sales force automation, retail point-of-sale, asset management, application development, and project management.

Christensen, Pamela

Pamela Christensen has 25 years experience in designing, re-engineering and implementing new processes and technologies in the field of IT support services. She is currently a national practice manager for e-Support and help desk consulting at CompuCom, a consulting services and outsourcing firm. She has worked with companies across the country, ranging from start-ups to Fortune 500s. Her consulting services have helped identify and implement changes that enabled gains in efficiency, customer satisfaction and support affordability. Pamela has also served as vice-president of programs for the Seattle Chapter of HDI for the past two years and is an HDI certified site auditor. Her well-rounded background in the IT field provides a wide range of expertise and experience.

Farver, Chris

As a senior consultant for Compuware Corporation, Chris provides help desk consulting for clients, outsourcing services for client help desks, and supplemental expertise for all levels of the help desk from entry-level analysts to senior managers. Chris has more than 20 years of experience in the IT industry focusing the past 14 years in the areas of networking technologies and the support industry. He speaks regularly at HDI Local Chapter meetings and industry events. Chris was a founding member of the North Coast Chapter of HDI in Cleveland in 1993 and has held officer positions for the past six consecutive years including two years as vice president of programs and four years as president of the chapter. During this time, the North Coast Chapter has received the International HDI's Chapter Excellence Award three times. Chris currently serves on the Help Desk Institute's Member Advisory Board as the Midwest Regional Director.

Fry, Malcolm

With more than 30 years of experience, Malcolm Fry is the world's foremost expert in service management and an Executive Partner with Peregrine Systems, Inc. (NASDAQ: PRGN), one of the world's leading software companies. He supports the company's thought-leadership platform in Infrastructure Management with a specific focus on service management. Mr. Fry is widely acknowledged for his work in developing service-management best practices, having authored four best-selling books and a video series for the help desk Institute. In addition, Mr. Fry is in continuous demand worldwide by the world's leading technology companies as a dynamic and entertaining speaker and knowledgeable advisor. During his career, Mr. Fry has lectured to more than one million people in more than 30 countries around the world. His dynamic, entertaining and innovative style enables him to communicate with diverse audiences. Mr. Fry is also an advisory board member of the help desk Institute Advisory Board.

Guy, Anna

Anna L. Guy is the help desk Manager at Blue Cross and Blue Shield of Florida, Inc. where she has been employed for 28 years. She is the founding president of the First Coast Local HDI Chapter in Jacksonville, Florida and is currently the Southeast Regional Director for the HDI Advisory Board. Anna's involvement with help desks began in 1986 when she implemented a help desk at Blue Cross and Blue Shield of Florida, Inc. She led many automation efforts for the Data Center (i.e. Automated Balancing, Automated Scheduling, Automated Report Distribution) and then spent a short time in a business unit where she learned how to manage a call center. After becoming manager of the help desk, she led her organization to become a "Best-in-Class" help desk. Anna is passionate about customer service, help desk, and HDI. When not working, you will find Anna busily involved in her other love, building an orphanage and school in Caberet, Haiti and leading Women's Ministries conferences across the state of Florida.

Holt, Donna

Returning for her second term as president, Donna is a founding member of the HDI Individual Certification Standards Committee, Certified HDA trainer, HDI Certified Site Auditor and help desk consultant. She is currently the Western

Regional Director of the HDI Advisory Board. Donna has been involved in every aspect of the help desk industry. Her business experience includes international trading, telecommunications, manufacturing, credit analysis and finance for several Fortune 500 companies during her thirty-year career. She has been an officer of the Orange County Local Chapter for six years.

Joslin, Richard

Richard "Rick" Joslin provides consulting services related to implementing and enhancing support operations with a key focus on knowledge management and e-service. Formerly, Rick was the VP of Customer Care for ServiceWare, which supports one of the most demanding audiences — customer service professionals. He also served as VP of RightAnswers.com and VP of Knowledge Engineering. A winner of the 1999 Service 25 Award, Rick has been widely acknowledged as one of the most influential luminaries in the support industry. Rick is the chairman of the Help Desk Institute's Member Advisory Board. He has been an active member of the Consortium for Service Innovation's Virtual Support Communities committee, serves on the Board of Advisors for the Help Desk Institute and the Indiana University of Pennsylvania's Business College, as well as an officer in the Pittsburgh Chapter of HDI.

LaBounty, Char

Char LaBounty is founder and President of LaBounty & Associates, Inc., a service management-consulting firm focused on the growing field of customer support services, dedicated to providing quality technology support practices that enhance client's business initiatives. Char is one of the preeminent experts on the development and application of service level management and service level agreements and writes and speaks extensively on the subject, throughout the world. Prior to her current position, she was the Director of the Membership Services Division for the Help Desk Institute. Char has over 20 years experience in the support industry as a line practitioner and is on the Advisory Boards of the Help Desk Institute, Key3Media's Support Service Events, and DCI Help Desk Professional Events and sits on the Editorial Board of United Publications IT Support News. Char is a much sought after speaker at computing and support events around the world, and has dedicated her career to providing sound customer service practices.

Mainarick, Lisa

Lisa is currently an Information Technology Manager for the City of Palo Alto, CA. She is responsible for overseeing the help desk and support staff as well as office automation, service level agreements, enterprise agreements and project management. Overall, Lisa has 5 years experience within information technology. Prior to her tenure with the City of Palo Alto, Lisa worked for the City of Milpitas in California for 6 years; 2 of which she provided as the Information Technology Customer Service Manger. Lisa is one of the founding members of the HDI Silicon Valley Chapter and serves as the VP of Programs for the chapter.

Peele, Lynn

Lynne Peele is currently the manger of Information Support Services at Unifi, Inc. in Greensboro North Carolina. Unifi is the largest producer of polyster-textured yarn in the United States. She recently revived the North Carolina TriadHDI and is the current president. Lynne has her Bachelors Degree in Business Administration and has been involved in the help desk industry for more than 10 years.

Rizzitano, Kim

Kim Rizzitano has been working in numerous areas of the help desk industry for over 13 years. She is a Certified Help Desk Manager, and is presently the Information Center Help Desk Manager at The MarMaxx Group. She has been a member of the Help Desk Institute for many years and over the past two years, she has been very active with the local New England Chapter first as VP of Membership, and presently as VP of Programs.

Sockrider, John

John Sockrider is a two-term president and past secretary of the Indiana Chapter of HDI. He is currently a self-employed training and computer support consultant. John was a senior analyst on the help desk at USA Group and Sallie Mae where he helped implement a large call and problem tracking system. Previously, he was an engineer and manager for 15 years in the telecommunications industry. He also has 15 years experience providing managerial, leadership, and technical training for many different groups.

Streitwieser, Jennifer

Jennifer has extensive experience in designing, planning, and implementing customer-focused service organizations. She has advised CEO's and CIO's on increasing the business benefit and improving the effectiveness of strategic customer service, technology, and e-business initiatives. Her background in technology and marketing enables her to help clients develop complete solutions that encompass sales, service and support.

Szymanski, Dick

Dick Szymanski is founder and general manager of Support Performance and a veteran of over 23 years in help desk, customer support and information technology. Known for his passion for customer service and creative influence in the area of industry standards, Dick founded CompareTM – The Support Industry Benchmark Database, served as a founding member of the Help Desk Institute Site Certification Standards Committee and in early 2000 qualified as one of the first HDI Certified Site Auditors in the world. Dick has performed and directed consulting projects for the improvement of customer support and help desk operations and conducted training and education for support managers and executives across the country since 1993. His previous exposure includes a prior 15 years of software design, development and implementation, project management and building and managing a software support center.

Whitman, Robin

Robin Whitman has over 10 years of experience in the help desk industry and server administration. A member of the Help Desk Institute New England Chapter for many years, Robin has held the position of VP Membership. Currently Robin holds the positions of president and treasurer for the Chapter.

Chapter

By Lynne Peele

Purposes and Objectives
of the Help Desk

For the purposes of this handbook, the term Help Desk means the part of the organization whose primary funtion is to answer questions and coordinate the resolution of problems, questions or service requests that customers encounter while using technical products and services. Customers of the Help Desk may be external clients of the company or internal customers, who are employees.

In addition to dealing primarily with technical products and services, Help Desks often act as a single point of contact for a broad range of support issues related to technical and non-technical corporate infrastructure support issues.

Sometimes known as technical support centers, customer support centers, contact centers, support services and IT support, to name a few, Help Desks have grown drastically over the last decade. Additionally, the scope of work and the positions of support organizations have greatly advanced.

In many organizations, the methods of providing help to customers evolved over the years as companies applied information processing to more and more functions. In some cases, customers had one number to call for hardware problems, another for software questions on the mainframe, another for PC questions, and possibly even a different number for teleprocessing or network problems.

In recent years, companies have followed the trend of consolidating the various customer support areas into one consolidated Help Desk organization or service desk. Providing a single point of contact for customers to report problems creates an audit trail of problem documentation and resolution, and a central repository of information for analysis and tracking.

Help Desk Activities

Help Desk activities have always had a primary focus on answering customers' questions, assisting with repairs, and facilitating service requests. The Help Desk resolves and/or coordinates the resolution of customer problems or acts as the liaison between the technical staff and the customer community.

From a customer's viewpoint, the Help Desk represents a single point of contact for support; this is true even if the resources required to address the customer's needs involves multiple support groups. Centralizing customer support helps ensure customer satisfaction because the customer no longer has to follow a problem as it passes to different support personnel.

When the customer community includes key customers or departments that require priority responses, the Help Desk ensures this level of service by commanding the appropriate resources. For the typical customer call, the Help Desk provides the first level of problem resolution—often the sole source of help required. While the typical Help Desk will resolve 70% plus of customer problems during the initial contact (from Help Desk Institute's 2001 Best Practices Survey), the results of this metric vary widely.

The Help Desk benefits the customer community in many ways beyond providing a single point of contact for support. These benefits are not always immediately apparent to individual customers. For example, by logging and tracking calls from all customers, the Help Desk is uniquely positioned to identify customers' training and education needs to further their knowledge and productivity. The Help Desk has a pivotal, often primary role in building self-help solutions that allow the customer to resolve many issues without impacting the support staff.

Besides aiding the customer community, the Help Desk serves as a valuable resource for the technical development staff. By documenting, assessing and routing problem calls, the Help Desk reduces the interaction between technical staff and customers, thereby increasing the technical staff's productivity.

Help Desk reporting of problem status and history can foster an overall improvement in the quality of service. Help Desks can provide trending information to management that would otherwise be unavailable, making earlier identification of problems possible and providing better data for root-cause analysis. In addition, by analyzing and addressing the root causes of problems, the Help Desk can help eliminate many of these problems as well as the calls they cause. For those problems and questions that are not eliminated, the Help Desk can develop knowledge management resources to allow quicker access to solutions in the future. When made directly available to customers, a knowledgebase can also reduce the cost of providing solutions.

The unique intermediary position the Help Desk holds also opens new possibilities for improving information-processing services throughout an organization. The Help Desk can identify customer requirements and service expectations; evaluate the effectiveness of products, vendors and staff; and compile and report these findings to the organization's management team.

In defining the purpose and objectives of your Help Desk—and establishing the staff and procedures to meet them—your organization can achieve a quality information-processing service that meets the current and future needs of your customer community.

Example Help Desk Mission Statement:
To maximize operational efficiency in the organization by providing timely resolution to information processing questions and effectively managing these problems to continuously improve the quality of the Help Desk service, system availability and the effectiveness of training.

Chapter

By Pamela Christensen

Organizing the Help Desk

If you are given the opportunity to build a new Help Desk or to re-engineer an existing support structure, you have a variety of design options available to you, depending on your customers' requirements, your budget, the culture of your business, the end users and the types of services you are expected to provide.

Whether you are building a Help Desk from scratch, consolidating a group of existing Help Desks or seeking ways to improve your support operations, this chapter can help. We will provide guidelines for how to structure your Help Desk and determine the support architecture to build a best-in-class operation that will efficiently provide high-value service to your company by increasing customer productivity. Key considerations include the pros and cons of a central-point-of-contact, consolidated Help Desk; whether to consolidate physically, logically or implement a virtual Help Desk; keeping your support in-house, outsourcing, or implementing a combination of both.

Management and Customer Requirements

The first step in designing or redesigning your Help Desk should always be to talk to your information services decision makers, managers and customers to identify their support requirements and expectations. It is also important to discuss funding strategies with the CIO, CFO or budget decision makers. Questions such as whether your support services will be charged back to your customers' business units, supported by high-level funding or paid for by some other method should be raised and addressed. Combining the customer requirements with the allocated funding and billing methods will provide you with the basis for your Help Desk design by establishing the requirements and cost constraints. With these two elements you have the skeleton around which you can begin designing the Help Desk.

After establishing the parameters within which you'll have to work, some sample questions that you will want to ask your sponsors and customers are:

- **What hours of support are required?**
  Staffing for a 24/7 operation is more difficult, for example, than staffing for a 12/5 operation.
- **What is the actual or projected volume of incidents? What is the projected volume during off-shifts and weekends?**
  The project volume of incidents will provide critical staffing information. If this is a new Help Desk or metrics are not available, industry-average figures can be used to project volumes. If it is expected that the number of incidents during off-hours will be relatively low, support options such as emergency pagers or using an outsource vendor for these times might be the most cost-effective solution.
- **What is the value of the incident, or what is the cost impact of an outage?**
  Often the outage of a particular application can result in millions of dollars of lost revenues. In these situations it is worth the expense of providing additional coverage to mitigate the risk of lost revenue in the event of an outage.
- **What products will be supported and what services will be provided by your Help Desk?**
  More and more Help Desks are evolving into full-service desks, providing change management, problem management, IMAC (Install, Move, Add, Change) support-asset management, configuration integrity, as well as other services.
- **How do your customers prefer to contact your Help Desk?**
  Current options have been expanded beyond the traditional phone call

and include voice mail, e-mail, Web chat, and Web-submitted requests that can integrate with your ACD system to initiate automatic callbacks.

• **What is an acceptable time to wait before your contact is answered?** In today's environment of multiple contact methods it is important to ask this question for each method of contact you plan to use. You may be expected to provide a 60-second call answer time, while a 2-hour response time for voice mail or e-mails may be acceptable. Keep in mind that the length of the response time will have a direct correlation on the cost of your service.

Once you have determined your customers' expectations and requirements and combine them with the budget and funding allocations, you have the baseline data you need to begin to design, consolidate or redesign your Help Desk.

To Outsource or Not to Outsource...That Is the Question
Today's rapidly changing environment, combined with information technology skill constraints and increasing salaries, is causing many companies to seek outsource service providers to support or augment the internal support structure. Outsourcing your Help Desk could be considered as an option to offset the expense and investment of building a support structure from scratch, to reduce the impact and costs of staff turnover, to provide the needed skills and expertise that your Help Desk staff doesn't have or to allow your business to focus on its core competencies. Your company may be looking for ways to better leverage its information technology assets, or simply looking to a vendor to provide a wider range of support. The table below illustrates some of the selection criteria to use to help determine if outsourcing is something that could be considered for your Help Desk:

Issue	Insource	Outsource	Combine	Benefit
High staff turnover		X		According to the Gartner Group, the cost of replacing staff is about $10,000. This cost includes recruiting, training, and human resources processing costs. Outsourcing moves the burden of staff replacement to the vendor.
High number of internally-developed line of business applications	X		X	Usually an internal Help Desk is more familiar with unique business processes and custom applications. However, if there is an adequate knowledgebase in place with support documentation, a vendor could adequately provide support for these applications. A combination of internal and outsource service providers could be considered.
Infrastructure not in place		X		It can be expensive to purchase the infrastructure for a best-in-class Help Desk. Outsourced vendors can spread these costs across multiple customers, reducing the cost of purchasing and supporting high-end technology.

Issue	Insource	Outsource	Combine	Benefit
The Help Desk role in the overall IT career path	X			Many companies use the Help Desk as a key step in an overall information technology career path. Help Desk analysts must become skilled in supporting multiple hardware and software platforms, making the Help Desk an ideal point to launch a career in information technology.
High volume of incidents for off-the-shelf software		X	X	Support for off-the-shelf software, such as Microsoft Office or Exchange, can be provided very efficiently by a vendor, enabling you to avoid the training and certification costs of maintaining those skills in-house. A combination of in-house and outsource services can reduce your staffing requirements by maintaining a small number of staff to handle the incidents for your line of business applications, while routing the calls for off-the-shelf software to a vendor.

Issue	Insource	Outsource	Combine	Benefit
24/7 support required		X	X	Depending on the volume and priority of calls received during off-hours, weekends and holidays, off-hour support can often be provided more efficiently and economically by an outsource vendor. Determining the right number of staff and finding people with the right skills who are willing to work off-shifts is difficult. Low volumes often make it impractical to require a physical presence at the Help Desk. By sharing resources with other customers, outsource vendors can provide skilled 24/7 support at a reduced cost.

Considerations for Consolidating the Help Desk

Consolidating multiple Help Desks into a single point of contact offers many benefits to your service partners and your customers. By successfully consolidating into a single point of contact, you can: lower your cost per incident by eliminating redundancy, reduce the number of staff required to maintain service levels; consolidate data to allow more accurate root-cause analysis and problem management; and improve customer satisfaction by improving consistency of support and improving response times. When planning a consolidation it isn't necessary to locate all staff in the same facility; it is actually preferred to have multiple locations to provide for fail-over, which allows you to staff more efficiently if you support customers in multiple time zones. Further savings can be realized by implementing a "virtual support center" using CTI technology to link them together, allowing analysts to telecommute. Whether you consolidate physically or logically, there are some key considerations to successfully implementing this model. First, it is essential that the person selected to manage the consolidated desk possess the right skills. According to the Gartner Group article "Pitfalls in Help Desk Consolidations" published November 17, 1999, the following management skills are required when managing a consolidated desk:

- Business knowledge
- Financial skills
- Leadership skills
- Internal and external negotiation skills
- Communication (i.e., written, verbal, presentation) skills
- Effective customer service skills
- Technology skills
- Training skills
- Quality-assurance skills

A good marketing and communication plan published to your customers and the support staff is critical to the success of the consolidation. Customers and support staff should be informed of the consolidation plan, how it will benefit them and the company as a whole, what the impacts are to them and when changes will occur. Once the plan is published, it is critical to execute it as communicated. Employees and end users will be less resistant to the changes if they understand the timeline and have an expectation of when the organizational and procedural changes will be completed.

Until recently, the quality and reliability of voice-over IP was unacceptable for the use of most Help Desks. However, with recent increases in quality of service standards, in a LAN or managed WAN environment, VoIP can be cost-effective and the quality on par with traditional voice. These strides have made implementing a single logical or "virtual" Help Desk a design that has many advantages over a physically consolidated Help Desk. The cost of implementing must be weighed against the benefits of this model, but a virtual Help Desk can also offer many soft cost advantages.

A virtual or logical consolidated desk from a customer's viewpoint is just like a standard Help Desk: they call a single phone number and the call is routed to an available analyst, either using skills-based routing or queuing. From their desktop, managers and administrators can manage the entire virtual center by accessing real-time reports, monitoring analysts' calls and analyzing historical trending data.

Structuring Your Help Desk

There's more to a Help Desk than having people available to answer the phone, and the days of a level-one support desk that does nothing more than triage are going the way of the dinosaur and the Edsel. Our support desks today are expected to respond to the customer in a manner of seconds whether the request comes via voice, e-mail or chat, and to quickly resolve the customer's problem during the initial contact or, at a minimum, gather and analyze enough data to diagnose the problem and get it to the right support partner who can resolve the problem. Our Help Desks are also expected to provide business value by identifying problem trends and eliminating recurring problems, to maintain ownership of critical outages until they are resolved, and to learn and use new technology to streamline the support process. Analysts who are the first point of contact for the customer are fully occupied with meeting service levels and resolving problems, with little time left to devote to supporting other tasks. Therefore, meeting additional expectations requires a support structure to the Help Desk to handle tasks such as:

• Problem management (tracking problem trends, root-cause analysis and problem resolution)
• Developing knowledge-management content and Help Desk training programs
• End-to-end management of critical outages, including an outage notification process
• Collecting data and reporting on service-level metrics
• Participating in change-management activities
• Implementing and sustaining Help Desk technologies, such as incident management systems, password reset tools, remote-control tools, and self-help and knowledge-management tools.

The introduction of E-Support has introduced a new level into the support model. Enabling end users to help themselves means that the problems that do require a Help Desk call are more complex. Therefore, maintaining a high first-call resolution rate requires analysts with a higher skill level. Figure 1 represents the structure of a traditional Help Desk, while Figure 2 demonstrates an E-Support Help Desk model.

Support to the Help Desk

Level 1
Entry-level or low-skill position responsible for
call receipt, call routing, problem diagnosis, some
problem resolution and problem escalation

Level 2
Higher-skilled position generally requiring some level of
certification. problem resolution over the phone or at
the desk, and problem escalation.

Level 3
Highly skilled network engineers, server administrators
and database administrators.
Top level of escalation.

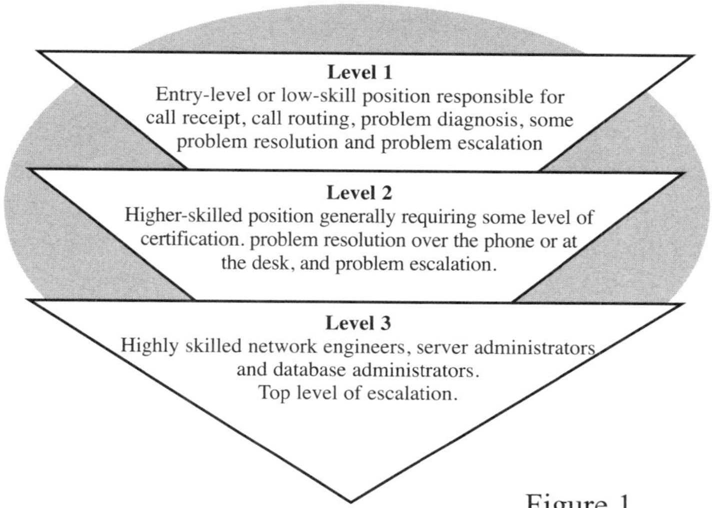

Figure 1

Support to the Help Desk

Level 0
Self-help, Self-healing portal. If customers cannot resolve the problem, it is escalated using a
predefined workflow to the
appropriately skilled analyst.

First Level of Contact
Combination of level 1 and level 2. Highly skilled
position requiring some level of certification.
Problem resolution over the phone, by e-mail or
chat. Use of remote-control tools to have more
insight into solving end user's problem.
Expected to solve most problems
without escalation and to
develop content for
the support portal.

Level of Escalation
Highly skilled network engineers, server administrators
and database administrators. Top level of
escalation. Expected to develop
troubleshooting and problem
resolution content for first level
of contact analysts

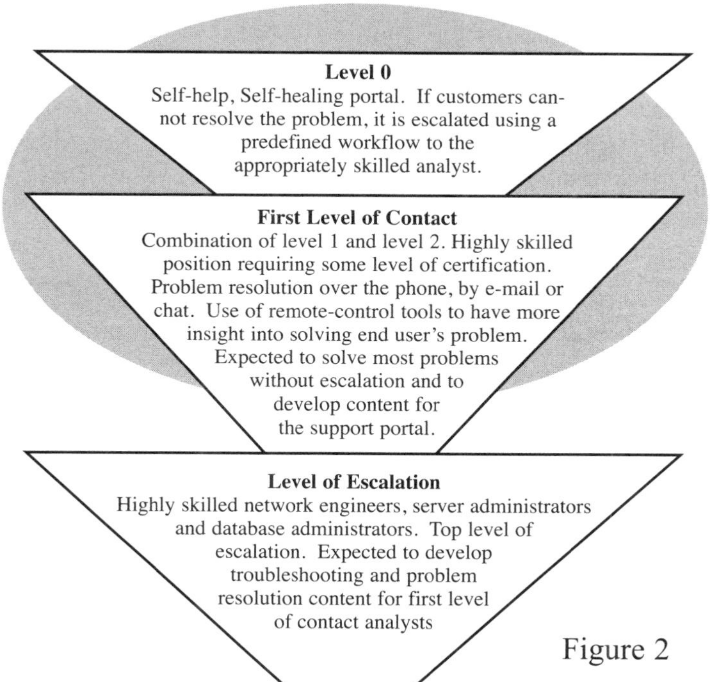

Figure 2

Customer Interface

Contacting the Help Desk used to be pretty cut-and-dried: either the Help Desk provided a phone number or it was located close enough for customers to walk over to ask for help. Today there are many choices to be considered in how you would like to provide your customers with access to your Help Desk. The traditional walk up and phone still are viable choices; you can also use voice mail, fax, e-mail, Web chat or a support portal that includes e-Support technology with an interface to contact a live person for help, as methods for your customers to request help. You can use one, some or all of these methods when building or re-engineering your Help Desk. The method you choose will depend on your budget, the size and culture of your customer base, the type of support you provide and the technology you have in place. Most Help Desks no longer have the luxury of simply accepting phone calls and walkups. But before implementing contact methods such as e-mail, Web or Web chat time, resources must be dedicated to developing the processes and workflows, additional analyst skills and training are required, SLA commitments for each method must be determined and you must identify how you will market and train your customer community on the new methods and service levels of each medium. Marketing and communication is critical to your customer's satisfaction level. For example, if the service commitment for responding to e-mail is 2 hours, send an automated e-mail response to the customer that clearly states this response time. This will ensure that your customer is not expecting an immediate response to the issue.

Web chat is becoming more and more common in Help Desks and offers the benefits of allowing your analyst to help more than one customer at a time, as well as enabling a mobile customer who is connecting over a phone line to talk to a live person without disconnecting from the modem. The disadvantages, however, include slow network response and dropped connections, which can increase the frustration of your customer who has to reconnect and then explain the problem from the beginning to a different support analyst. Analysts providing written customer support require different skills than those providing voice support; therefore, it is important to provide training on effective business writing to those analysts who will be supporting chat and e-mail queues.

E-Support portals integrate self-help technology, such as password reset and knowledge bases, with your call-tracking system to provide a convenient way for end users to solve their own problems. E-Support portals also make it easy for users to contact the Help Desk either by allowing them to submit a support request from the portal, or by including the ability to initiate a support call or chat session. Introducing a support portal as a method of enabling your customers to help themselves—therefore eliminating calls to the Help Desk—can significantly reduce the cost of support and can increase customer productivity. Support portals do require a robust maintenance process to ensure the data is kept up to date and is relevant to the problems that are being experienced. A support portal that is not maintained will not be used, resulting in not only the loss of a significant investment in time and resources, but an adverse affect on the reputation of the Help Desk.

Communication Within the Help Desk

Each one of the analysts on the Help Desk is your contact with the customer and must be enabled to resolve problems quickly and efficiently while presenting a professional and courteous face to customers. To achieve this, they need to be kept informed of all the information that impacts their ability to provide support. In a 24/7 Help Desk, getting information to everyone is no easy challenge. The risks of not keeping everyone involved and informed are high, ranging from low morale and high employee turnover, to analysts providing inaccurate or obsolete information to your customers. The table below provides some suggestions to keep your Help Desk staff informed, without comprising your ability to meet service levels.

Method	Challenge	Suggestion
Staff meetings	In most Help Desks, the entire staff cannot be tied up in a staff meeting at the same time. Multiple shifts create even more of a challenge.	By watching trends in contact volumes, staff meetings can be scheduled during times that are traditionally slow. Calls can be routed to voice mail for short periods, with a pager notification in the case of a critical outage. To support multiple shifts, and in large or high-volume Help Desks, multiple staff meetings must be held.
Physical and Web bulletin boards	Finding the time to keep bulletin boards up to date can be difficult in the high-volume, high-stress environment of most Help Desks. If the information on the board is not kept current, employees will cease to refer to the Web page or the physical board.	Make keeping the board up to date a priority. Consider creating a communications team with the charter to post information that is not only critical to share, but also fun, such as birthdays, quotes of the week, etc.
Newsletters and e-zines	In the hectic environment of a Help Desk, publishing newsletters takes second priority to putting out the fire of the moment.	Consider publishing newsletters and e-zines quarterly. Offer incentives to analysts who submit articles and share information. Make it mandatory that system changes scheduled for the coming quarter be published in the newsletter.

Method	Challenge	Suggestion
Reader boards	The challenge is capturing information in a meaningful, concise form. Obviously, in Help Desks that are highly dispersed or virtual, traditional reader boards don't work.	For traditional Help Desks where everyone is located in close proximity, the reader board offers a good tool to broadcast up-to-the-minute statistics and outage information. Developing templates for information improves the quality of the message and reduces the time involved composing and posting the message. In virtual or highly dispersed Help Desks, a Web-based reader board is a good solution.
Shift-change meetings	Developing the discipline to create the shift report and keep the meetings concise.	Create a standard agenda and templates for the shift reports

Chapter 3

By Lisa Mainarick

Physical Help Desk Arrangements

Feng Shui For Help Desks?

"Feng what?" you ask. Feng shui (pronounced "feng SHWAY") is an ancient Chinese philosophy that, in its simplest form, says your surroundings affect your energy. One does not have to believe in the feng shui philosophy, but many of the basic principles generally apply and are quite practical to Help Desks and work environments.

Overview

The physical arrangement of a Help Desk can greatly affect the productivity of its support staff. Therefore, it becomes imperative to create a positive working environment that encourages productivity, decision-making and knowledge transfer. In this chapter, we will discuss how physical arrangements combined with specialized tools can lead to a successful feng shui Help Desk.

Office

If at all possible, try to situate Help Desk staff in one common office. An office with a door, situated in close proximity to second- and third-level technical staff, is most effective. This arrangement works best because cubicle noise or foot traffic will not disrupt the Help Desk staff while on the phone. This separate office also encourages more open communication, brainstorming sessions and increased team spirit among Help Desk staff. Moreover, this separate office becomes vital in the event of a major problem or crisis because it allows Help Desk staff to quickly converse, strategize and execute an effective action plan.

Desk

From a feng shui perspective, the positioning of one's desk is an essential element to maintaining concentration and lowering stress levels—two very important factors while working on a Help Desk. Desks should be arranged facing the door while sitting; this will lessen vulnerability to surprises and allow for better concentration. If facing the door is not an option, consider placing a small mirror positioned towards the doorway for clear visibility of who is entering. The mirror can also serve as a reminder to smile when speaking on the phone. Customers on the other end of the line may not be able to see that smile, but they can certainly hear it in the Help Desk agent's voice.

Lighting

Wherever possible, allow natural light to come into the office. Do not close off windows with shades or curtains. Where artificial light supplements natural light, ensure it is gentle and indirect and does not cause glare on computer monitors. Although lights are extremely wonderful energizers, overhead lighting in an office generally is not enough. Therefore, a good desk lamp for a work area will help bring in energy and aid in better concentration and focus. Also, if natural light is not an option, painting the walls a light oak color with a non-reflective finish is recommended; this will help limit reflections from walls.

Ergonomics and Feng Shui

Help Desk staff should be viewed as the nucleus of any technology department: They have the highest interaction with customers and deal with a variety of customer types. Therefore, it is necessary to invest in their comfort and well-being. With extended periods sitting while on the phone, it is important that ergonomics are taken into careful consideration. A well-designed chair is one investment that can go a long way. A chair should provide good mid- and lower-back support, as well as a back rest and seat that are independently adjustable. This will allow for controlled pressure on the thighs and back and ultimately increase productivity and reduce the potential for back injury.

Because Help Desk support requires one to have phone conversations while simultaneously operating a computer or other equipment, telephone headsets are highly recommended. Cradling a telephone handset between the ear and shoulder is usually uncomfortable, even with a shoulder rest. Tension and soreness can build up in the neck, shoulder and upper back, and if prolonged, this tension and soreness may result in repetitive strain injuries.

Also, to help prevent any repetitive stress injuries, a computer keyboard and mouse should be ergonomically friendly, with curvy shapes that benefit the flow of energy through fingers and hands. According to feng shui masters, energy flows most beneficially over curves rather than 90-degree angles and straight lines.

Bringing Nature Into the Office

A major element of feng shui is water. Actually, the meaning of "shui" is water. Water is considered to tap auspicious good fortune and success. Desk water fountains have certainly become a big hit in the local stores these days. It is no wonder these calming babbling brooks are such a hit, considering the amount of stress that comes with working in the high-tech world. However, it is important to note that according to feng shui masters, one should sit facing the water. Having water behind you can bring misfortune. Another way to bring nature into the office is the utilization of plants because they help energize with wonderful aromas that might otherwise be a very stale atmosphere.

6 Tips for Office Feng Shui

- Clean up any unnecessary clutter – this is conducive to relaxation,because it lessens the stress produced by the inability to find things
- Situate desks facing the door – this will allow for better concentration
- Sit away from drafts – not only does it affect the flow of energy,

but drafts can cause one to be more susceptible to illness
- Bring in some plants – not only do plants provide more oxygen in a room (which is often needed!), they help one stay connected with nature as well; an important element of feng shui
- Think curves - use office equipment that provides optimum comfort and fluid style for positive energy flow in the room. Avoid sharp angles or straight lines
- Add energizing colors or matted pictures representing teamwork, attitude, and encouragement. These positive affirmations can go a long way.

Specialized Help Desk Tools

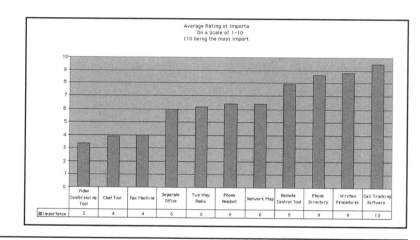

Figure 3-1   Graph from Help Desk survey conducted in August 2001 showing average level of importance of Help Desk tools

Although feng shui does not play a role in these specialized tools, many of these tools can assist in the well-being, efficiency and concentration of Help Desk staff. In a Help Desk survey conducted in August 2001, Help Desk managers and analysts were asked to rate the level of importance of various Help Desk tools on a scale of 1-10 (10 being most important). Call Tracking Software was the only tool that received an average rating of 10 (most important). A final question was asked: "Of the 11 tools listed, which do you feel is the most important for a Help Desk to be successful?" Only three of the tools were chosen: call tracking software, documentation and remote control.

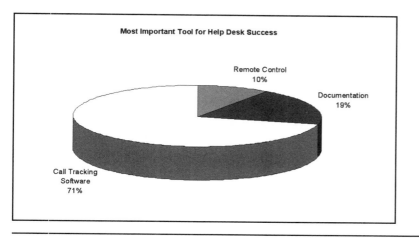

Chart identifying what tools are most important for Help Desk success.   Figure 3-2

Feng Shui All the Way or Feng Shui No Way?

Regardless if one chooses to accept the feng shui philosophy, many of the feng shui principles are common sense and already play a part in one's life. After all, anything that can increase productivity, is visually appealing and encourages harmony within, cannot be overlooked. Implementing these techniques into a Help Desk environment can ensure that the Help Desk staff is happy, which results in a better experience for the customer.

Chapter

By Lynn Albright

Staffing the Help Desk

In order to create an effective and successful Help Desk you need to first determine your staffing needs, then put together a team of specialists who can provide exceptional service to your customers while helping the organization meet its goals.

This chapter discusses how to determine your staffing needs, what skills and personality traits are important for a successful Help Desk. We'll give you ideas on training Help Desk specialists, team building and how to avoid stress and burnout.

How To Determine Staffing needs

Before you can determine what your staffing needs will be, you first need to define what your Help Desk functions are. Some of these functions could include:
• Answering incoming calls
• Tracking calls
• Analyzing and trouble shooting
• Resolving calls
• Ensuring customer satisfaction
• Closing calls

Help Desk Skills

It is important to hire individuals with the appropriate skills and personal characteristics to make your Help Desk a success. The technical skills required depends on the level and type of service your Help Desk provides, and the complexity of the problems you receive. Most organizations require Help Desk personnel to possess, at a minimum, general computer knowledge and troubleshooting ability. Other required skills will also depend upon the level and type of service provided. Some of those skills include: customer service skills, higher level of technical skills, and someone who possess integrity, independence, organization, and flexibility.

The required technical skills can be quantified analyzing your Help Desk's call history; the number of calls for different types of problems will reveal the skills required of your Help Desk analysts.

The level of automation your Help Desk uses to track calls also influences needed skills. Call tracking and analysis can also help define skill requirements and the number of personnel needed to staff the Help Desk. Analyze the number of total calls and calls by employee. Using call automation and tracking, information such as number of calls handled by time of day, day of week, agent, time spent on calls, and rolled and abandoned calls, will help to determine your staffing requirements. Don't forget to include absences such as sick leave, vacation and holidays.

When you evaluate your staffing requirements, compare call trends by type and actual performance to your service level commitments and staffing levels.

Personality Traits

The task of hiring Help Desk analysts has been a difficult one. Technical candidates often do not possess customer service skills and vice versa. Often it isn't apparent that you've hired the wrong person until after they have been through training and on the job for a few weeks. An employee screening assessment tool is available to assist Help Desk managers in identifying superior help desk professionals and promising candidates for Help Desk positions. HDI's Professional Aptitude Coaching Tool (PACT) provides valuable in-depth information about job candidates and will help hiring managers conduct a more in-depth interview based on the findings of the assessment.

Job Descriptions

Job descriptions vary among organizations and are based on departmental needs. Job descriptions should clearly define job functions, normal working hours, the qualifications needed, the level of experience and personality traits needed. Below is an example:

Summary Description

Always start your job description with a brief description summarizing the role of the analyst

Job Functions

List the functions of the job here

Qualifications and experience

Include everything here that you are looking for in an analyst. Be sure to add the required personality traits

Training

Training is the key to success for your Help Desk. Typically, though, Help Desk analysts tend to be trained on-the-job. This approach assumes analysts can quickly absorb all the skills necessary to do the job well. Frequently, this type of training results in inadequately trained people serving as the central point of contact between your information services group and the rest of the organization
There are a variety of training courses available in many types of media that can help. These include computer based training (CBT's), hands on mentoring, video training, off-site classroom training. HDI offers many of these types of training products and courses. Except for hands-on training, it is best to get your trainee away from the Help Desk environment during training periods. There are too many distractions that can occur, which will disrupt the learning process.

Type of Training

Training is vitally important to the success of your Help Desk. When given high priority, training pays off with many benefits to the information services department, the Help Desk staff, the customer community and the corporation. Training at your Help Desk should be a continuing process. As technology changes and new applications are developed, ongoing education can help both you and your Help Desk meet your customers' needs.

General Training

There are several areas in which training is needed, including telephone and listening skills, customer services, stress management, time management, listening, thinking, writing skills, typing, and problem solving skills. To establish a training plan for your Help Desk, assess strengths and weaknesses in these areas.

Technical Training

The type of technical skills you or your staff needs is site specific. If your goal is to resolve 95% of all reported problems, then your staff will need to obtain greater technical skills than if your objective were more modest.

Some technical training can include network management, hardware troubleshooting, customer service class, software applications, company-specific hardware, software and device configurations.

Team Building

Team building is essential to the success of your Help Desk. A successful team can provide multiple benefits to the customer community and overall organization. Help Desk analysts do not need to possess identical abilities, but should have, and foster, certain team building traits such as flexibility, open mindedness, people orientation, professional attitude, good communication skills, positive outlook, creativity and, probably most of all, lots of patience and empathy.

Individuals working as a team, support each other and work to help others accomplish the Help Desk's goals.

To develop a team that works together, the manager has to support the Help Desk 100% and reward the group as a team. Support should be verbal but can also include, budgeting for adequate salaries, making training available, making sure they have the most current technology to do their jobs, and holding meetings on a regular basis to keep them informed. Always take the time to hear their ideas and suggestions as well as complaints.

Chapter 5

*By Chris Broome and
Jennifer Streitwieser*

What is E-support

The support industry, like many industries, is subject to trends: from centralized support, to outsourcing, to expert systems to certifying employees. However, e-support—the biggest trend in recent years—is likely to revolutionize our industry as completely as the telephone did. More and more help desks are using e-support to provide better, faster customer service...all at reduced costs.

So what is e-support? There are multiple definitions, some of which focus on individual aspects or forms of support, such as PC remote control, the ability to input requests and check problem status via the Web, and using online chat as a means of call handling. Other definitions are much broader, describing e-support as the tools, processes and behaviors any 21st century help desk must have to be considered best-in-class. For purposes of this discussion, e-support is any customer interaction using the Internet or Web as the primary support communication channel. This includes:

- Customer self-help. Customers can access knowledgebases—perhaps the same ones your analysts use—to resolve problems. Or you may provide FAQs (as opposed to a complete knowledgebase) to deal with common, easily answered questions. Customers may have the option of downloading and installing approved software, or of finding updated drivers and patches. Additionally, you can provide tools for such things as password resets.

- Web requests. Your problem-management system may provide Web access, which allows customers to enter new requests, check the status of open calls or close calls that have been resolved. Consider providing an online satisfaction survey to capture whether calls have been resolved to the customer's satisfaction.
- E-mail and chat. These communication mechanisms offer an alternative to the telephone, which some customers may prefer. These methods have the added benefit of preserving the entire interaction in writing, enabling customers to refer to instructions again as needed.
- Remote control. You may have less-than-fond memories of talking a customer through editing AUTOEXEC.BAT, or saying, "No, don't hit 'Enter' yet!" Tools that give you control over your customers' PCs via a LAN have been around for quite a while, and remote-control Web tools are becoming common. You can see what your customers see, correct problems in far less time than a phone call would take and deliver on-the-spot training when needed.

Benefits of E-support

If e-support initiatives are implemented correctly, you improve customer service and you decrease operating costs. How does this happen?

Improving customer service

You improve customer service by giving customers more control. Which would you prefer:

- Firing off a quick e-mail at midnight when a question occurs to you, or waiting until 9:00 a.m. to call a Help Desk?
- Generating an online chat request that waits in the background and alerts you when a technician is available, or attempting to continue working with the phone clenched between your ear and shoulder and hold music echoing in your head?

Additional communication methods result in customer convenience and control. You improve customer service by empowering and educating your customers. With the advent of the Web, people are becoming used to searching for—and finding—information on any topic that strikes their fancy. By giving customers access to your information in the form of knowledgebases or FAQs, you give them both convenience and the pleasant sense of accomplishment that comes from solving a problem or learning something new.

Furthermore, you improve customer service by speeding up the time to resolve problems. Waiting on hold takes time. Talking someone through a problem or dispatching a technician takes more time. All of the forms of e-support can dramatically reduce the time it takes to move your customer from problem to solution.

Improving operating costs

E-support doesn't just benefit your customers. While you may incur additional infrastructure costs, depending on the current state of your systems, the return on investment for many e-support initiatives can be realized within one year of implementation. Benefits include:

- *Speeding up resolution time.* Every year for the past 10 years, most respondents to the Help Desk Institute's Practices Survey have said that their call volume is increasing. By decreasing resolution times, you can handle more calls with the same number of personnel. You can even free up some of your staff for training or proactive work.
- *Enhanced knowledge sharing.* Setting up knowledgebases for your customers means that your information needs to be accurate and complete. The very act of implementing a customer knowledgebase can lead to better-trained and better-informed technicians.
- *E-support is a two-way street.* Not only can your customers reach you, but you can reach your customers. You can quickly communicate the status of ongoing, systemwide problems via e-mail, provide project updates on the Web and correct problems before they generate a phone call by using remote control.
- *Cost savings.* Your average cost per call depends on your industry, type of Help Desk, services provided and a host of other factors. Average cost per transaction can range from 25 cents for a Web self-help transaction, to $20 for e-mail, to more than $100 for telephone support…and everything in between. There may be no consensus on what constitutes an "average" average, but the general trend is pretty clear: e-support lowers your cost per call. By allowing customers to help themselves and by increasing the efficiency of your staff (through

the use of remote control tools), employees can spend more time working on complex issues. And if your call volume increases, you may not need to increase the size of your staff…thus saving on direct staffing costs and overhead.

Is E-support Right for You?

Not every element of e-support is right for every Help Desk. You may get frequent calls that involve hardware repair, or have customers who prefer the reassuring sound of a human voice or the sight of a technician at their deskside. Some of the factors you should evaluate when considering e-support are:

- *Do your service calls lend themselves to e-support?* If you deal with a high percentage of calls involving how-to questions, basic service requests or password resets, e-support can help your customers help themselves. When it comes to handling move/add/change requests and systemwide outages, customers can make requests via the Web or e-mail, but you're probably going to have to go deskside or rely on field technicians to complete many requests. And while you can communicate status via the Web, if your customers don't have Web access you'll need to answer the calls! Finally, calls that have to do with actual hardware repair or other break/fix issues may also involve an onsite visit or a live conversation.

- *Are your customers ready for e-support?* Many people love the convenience of ATMs and self-service gas pumps, but there are also people who prefer to be waited on. You may have a customer base that is less technologically adept or not used to using the Internet for research or other types of interactions. For internal Help Desks, the corporate culture is important: if the emphasis is on personal service, you may need to move more slowly when considering e-support.

- *Do you have the resources available to develop and maintain quality e-support systems?* You can't just toss a pile of documentation on the Web and expect your customers to read it. (After all, most of us don't read our manuals or Help files!) Nor can you allow customers to send you e-mails and let your telephone staff respond to them "in their spare time." You need to set up the right processes and tools and work to maintain the efficacy of those processes and tools every single day.

• *Will e-support be better than your current methods of support?* If you won't be able to resolve a significant percentage of your calls, if your customers won't adapt to self-service mechanisms, if you don't have the resources to build and maintain good processes, then e-support probably isn't right for you. In fact, in some environments e-support may generate more calls than it will resolve, will encourage the use of workarounds as opposed to true resolutions, or will hide systemic problems that deserve more attention. Depending on your support operation, you may also find that e-support isn't any faster or more convenient from the customer's perspective than the services you already provide.

Getting Started

Assuming that you can answer yes to all of the questions posed thus far, how do you successfully implement e-support in your organization? Return to first principles: ensuring that the customer is central to the strategy. There is no point in engaging in a service improvement project if the customer doesn't benefit from the change. While many service initiatives are designed around improving internal processes, you have to make sure this translates into real improvements for your customers.

Providing e-support goes beyond selecting a tool. You also need to examine your processes, training curriculum, available skill sets, staff schedule and service levels, as well as gauge the impact of redesigning these to meet your goals. The five core areas listed below provide a framework for establishing your approach.

Strategy

• *Analyze your current support environment and determine where e-support fits in your overall strategy.* Consider the topics already discussed: the nature of your service requests, the types of customers you support, and how e-support will improve your service and your operations.
• *Gauge expectations.* Will your first phase include submitting Web requests, checking status online, searching FAQs, or all of the above? Does providing e-support mean you will now be available 24/7? What are the implications of any of these decisions?

- *Gain alignment*. You need to have internal agreement about the direction of the initiative. Different parts of your company may have different ideas about how to best implement or benefit from a service improvement project. More than just achieving buy-in, alignment sets expectations and points the way to internal satisfaction.
- *Create a cross-functional team to plan and develop your e-support initiative*. Determine who has ownership of each component. Some people may want to work on tool administration and integration, others on content creation and approval, and still others on process redesign. Make sure everyone understands his or her role and how the work each individual is doing links to the work of the rest of the team.
- *Build in continuous improvement from the beginning*. The information you make available to your customers won't be static—you'll need to update FAQs, add knowledgebase entries, upgrade remote-control tools. The process for doing these things should be designed early in your initiative.

Service Delivery

- *Focus on service levels*. Do you currently commit to specific turn-around times for problem-management and status requests? Will e-support change these in any way? Some service centers have different turnaround times for e-mail requests and phone requests. Whatever you decide, make sure you are consistent and can meet your commitments.
- *Diagram your call-handling process*. Are e-support requests handled in the same manner as phone requests? Track the life of an e-support request from the moment a customer submits it through its completion. Make sure you identify who is responsible for service delivery at each step—you don't want an e-mail sitting in a queue or inbox for days without an owner.
- *Focus on communication. E-support delivery is, by its nature, less personal than a live interaction*. Focus on ways you can keep communication flowing between you and your customers. The simplest techniques are autoresponse e-mails that let customers know you have received their message. Incorporate your e-support requests into your existing customer follow-up routines.

Standards

- *Determine your benchmarks*. Decide up front how you are going to evaluate the success of your e-support initiative. You want to be able to demonstrate that you have improved customer service and/or decreased operating costs. Therefore, it's important to take baseline measurements now of your customer satisfaction results and current operating costs, so when you have future statistics you can benchmark them against your starting point.
- *Evaluate your data*. If you are going to let your customers check their call status online, is the data in your call tracking system ready for prime time? Do you have accurate client data so customers can look themselves up in your database? Are your status codes easily understood by people who don't use them every day? Take a good look at the quality of your information and recategorize your information so it's easy for your customers to use.
- *Establish standard operating procedures*. Make sure you understand not only how e-support calls will be handled, but also how behind-the-scenes activities such as knowledgebase maintenance and tool configuration are going to happen.

Systems

- *Understand the existing functionality in your tools*. Many support tools already contain modules that you can use to build your e-support capability. Other modules are available with upgrades—talk to your tool vendors about this.
- *Evaluate your infrastructure needs*. Understand what you need in terms of e-mail accounts, intranet capabilities and integration with other systems. You can capitalize on your relationships with the other technical groups in your company to get what you need.
- *Configure your systems*. Take what you've learned from diagramming your call handling, service level and staffing needs, and determine what you have to change in your call tracking system and other tools. You may need new queues, priority codes, categories and a host of other fields. You will also need to design screen layouts and forms for your customers and support analysts.

Staff

- *Identify new skills for e-support*. Handling calls via e-mail and the Web requires excellent written communication skills. Do you know whether your support analysts use proper spelling and grammar? Devise an evaluation to determine which members of your staff are best suited to handling calls in this manner. The use of remote-control software requires extreme care and fastidious operation: causing your own computer to crash is unpleasant, but crashing a customer's PC can be a disaster!

- *Build your new schedule.* Many groups have found it useful to split phone calls and e-mail requests into different queues, handled by different groups, and then rotate the support analysts through these different roles. That way, the analyst can be more focused. This also allows analysts with stronger verbal skills to specialize in phone support and those with stronger written skills to specialize in e-support. However you choose to do this, you will need to rethink your daily schedule to ensure adequate coverage for all calls.

- *Train your group.* Your staff must be proficient in using the new tools you're making available to your customers. Make sure your group is aware of all the changes that will occur—changes to the call tracking system, to knowledgebases, to schedules, to standard operating procedures, etc.

Going Live

- *Pilot the change.* Before announcing your new initiative to your entire customer base, pilot with a select group so you can work out the kinks. This can also help you collect some initial data about the types and durations of calls you receive, thereby improving your forecasting.

- *Market your new service.* Your entire company is affected—directly or indirectly—by a change in customer service. Everyone should be aware of what is happening and why, and be ready to cheer you on!

- *Ongoing maintenance.* E-support requires constant effort. Incorporate tasks into the daily responsibilities of your staff, including keeping your content accurate and up to date, and incorporating customer feedback into your service delivery.

At the end of the day, e-support is simply "support"—it's all about the customer. E-support provides customers another way to interact with you and gives you another way to provide customer service. By ensuring you have all the bases covered when you implement your e-support initiative, you can improve both service delivery and your bottom line.

Chapter

By Diana Best

Call Handling—Moments of Truth

Any opportunity an organization has to form a positive or negative impression in the customer's mind is called a moment of truth. No information services group has more moment-of-truth opportunities than the Help Desk.

As the first point of contact for customers, the impression you leave with customers is key to their perception of the information services group and, possibly, of the entire company.

Impressions are often based less on what you say and more on how you say it. Therefore, this chapter emphasizes how to manage those critical interactions. First, we'll focus on basic telephone skills, and how both your equipment and tone of voice can impact your customer service. We'll also provide tips on improving your customer interaction and listening skills.

We'll address customer relationships, understanding customer needs and developing the art of negotiation. Finally, we'll learn how to recognize and manage the various customer behavior styles.

Basic Telephone Skills
The telephone skills you need at the Help Desk encompass using

the telephone equipment, controlling your tone of voice, interacting with your customers on a professional basis and learning to listen—really listen—to your customers.

Using the equipment:

Agents should be comfortable with their telephone equipment. Be sure you can easily transfer calls, place calls on hold and set up conference calls, if these functions are available. Practice using these functions before you need them.

Answer the phone in as few rings as practical; less than three rings is preferable. You may program the telephone equipment to automatically forward calls to another agent after a certain number of rings.

When using the telephone, position the mouthpiece directly in front of your mouth. Using telephone headsets ensures correct placement of the mouthpiece while freeing the agent's hands and neck. Speaking on a telephone requires better articulation than conversing face to face because there is no visual communication.

You may have telephone equipment that allows the customer to listen to music or a radio station while waiting. While this can ease the stress of waiting, it's better to give customers information regarding current average hold times, so they can anticipate the delay. [Specialized equipment and software is available to calculate and announce expected hold times for you. You may also be able to set up a preliminary announcement about current problems, before the call is forwarded to you. Many people will call to be sure you are aware of a problem, and will be reassured to hear you are already working on it.]

If you are eating or drinking something when the telephone rings, swallow and wait a few seconds before answering.

Tone of voice:

The inflection of your voice is important. It can convey sincerity, humor, sarcasm, skepticism and many other shades of meaning. Make sure you communicate what you intend.

```
┌─────────────────────────────────────────────┐
│   Factors that control voice quality:         │
│                                               │
│       1. Energy                               │
│       2. Rate of speech                       │
│       3.Pitch                                 │
│                                               │
└─────────────────────────────────────────────┘
```

Three factors that affect voice quality   Figure 5-1

Figure 5-1 presents the three factors that affect the quality of your voice: energy, rate of speech and pitch. Your energy level reflects attitude and enthusiasm. Your rate of speech needs to be at a moderate level—typically 125 words per minute. Faster speaking may create problems, and speaking too slowly can convey the impression of patronizing the customer. You can vary the pitch of your voice by modulating your tone and inflection. Listen to your customer and let them be your guide for the rate of speed and technical level you use.

If you smile when answering the telephone, your voice will actually sound friendlier. This can have a big impact on how the customer feels about you and the Help Desk.

Customer Contact

You may never meet many of your customers face to face; you'll know them only through the telephone. After greeting the caller, identify your department's name and yourself, unless your company has a policy against this.

Suggested greeting: "Good afternoon. This is the Help Desk, Mary speaking. How may I help you?"

Note the customer's name and use it several times during the call. People like the sound of their name, so it holds their attention. Different customs prevail at different companies and in different countries, but generally use first names to personalize the conversation. However, don't be too informal. Be consistent. All analysts should use the same script when answering the phone.

If you need to place a customer on hold, ask for permission and wait for an answer. Never leave a person on hold for more than 30 seconds without checking back. Never hold a conversation with another person in your area without putting the customer on hold. Putting your hand over the mouthpiece is no guarantee that you won't be overheard.

Keep track of who is holding on each line. Avoid questions such as, "Whom are you holding for?" Other statements to avoid include: "I don't know where Steven is, but I'll have him call you when he gets back," and "She is in the middle of a big problem right now." These statements tell customers two negative things: their problems are not perceived as big, and they must wait in line for Help Desk analysts to solve other problems.

You should be able to access basic information related to the customer very quickly. Ideally this customer information would be on a PC or mainframe database. Or, it could be as simple as a box of index cards or a Rolodex file with basic information recorded. Quick access is important, but maintaining thorough, current information is also critical. For this reason, it is vastly preferable to get beyond paper-based systems—which are difficult to update—and use a computerized system that automatically updates information as your organization makes network and configuration changes.

Learning to Listen

Listen carefully. This sounds obvious, but it's still the most important lesson for analysts to learn. If you don't listen carefully, you will hear what you expect to hear; callers will pick up on this and your credibility will be lost. Although it can be an important time-saver to identify recurring problems with similar solutions, each problem has the potential of being unique. Ask specific questions to separate the unusual from the routine.

Once you document the details of a problem, affirm the importance of the problem to the caller. For example, use the caller's words whenever possible: "I understand that not receiving that information is delaying the completion of your weekly report. We'll try to find out what happened as quickly as possible."

Controlling the Call

You can also improve your telephone techniques by using open-ended and closed-ended questions, seeking expert help when necessary, ending your conversations by getting agreement from your customers and making follow-up calls to certain customers when necessary.

Types of Questions

When you want to encourage customers to speak freely, use open-ended questions—questions they can't answer with a yes or no. For example, instead of asking, "Has the problem negatively impacted your area?" ask, "How would you describe the impact of this problem on your area?"

When you want to limit the range of customers' responses to a choice, use closed-ended questions. For example: "We can get someone there quickly. Will 2:00 this afternoon be OK?"

You often need to use open-ended questions at the start of a call to learn the necessary details. These questions usually start with: who, what, when, where, why and how.

Closed-ended questions can help you gain agreement and limit the length of a conversation. They often start with: did, can, have, do, is, will and would.

Getting Additional Help

Most Help Desks today don't refer customers to their support partners. Problems that cannot be resolved at the Help Desk are re-assigned by the Help Desk analyst to the support partners, who will contact the customer. In the past, customers became frustrated when they were referred to a second and third person, especially if they couldn't reach them immediately or if they were referred to the wrong person. Having the Help Desk route the problem to the support partner who can best resolve it ensures that the Help Desk remains the single point of contact for your customers.

Ending the Conversation

Conversations can often take many paths and can become confusing when it comes to what is expected of whom. At the end of your conversation, briefly summarize the problem, the planned actions and the timing of those actions. This ensures both parties agree and understand each other.

Tell the customer the reference number you assigned to the problem, and encourage the customer to make a note of it. It will save both parties time during future discussions about the problem.

Always thank customers for calling, ask them if they need any additional help and encourage them to call again. The customer will remember the end of the conversation more than any other segment. Let the customer hang up first; this gives the customer a final chance to say something.

Follow-up

Whatever follow-up actions you commit to, it's critical to document these activities in the call record and then carry out these actions. This is particularly important with promised callbacks, since customers often have to wait in queue to reach an agent and will resent explaining the situation again.

In many cases, analysts will have dispatched a support partner as follow-up to a call. In that case, it is the analyst's responsibility to track the level of service provided by the support partners to ensure they reach the site as promised and work within the service-level agreements. Realistically this is often difficult, but it must be accomplished, even after the fact if necessary, because the customer has no point of accountability other than the Help Desk.

Customer Relationships

Vanderbilt University coach Red Sanders is attributed with saying, "Winning isn't everything, it's the only thing." Similarly, customer service is the only thing for the Help Desk; it has no other reason to exist. Serving your customers means making them feel good about moment-of-truth transactions. Beyond the basics of call handling, the Help Desk must strive to build a rapport and good reputation with its customer community. A reputation is built over time. If that reputation is less than satisfactory, it will take time to change it, but it can certainly be done.

Some key areas to focus on when building customer relationships include understanding customers' needs, creating a customer liaison, the art of negotiation, recognizing and managing customer behavior, and accentuating the positive.

Understanding the Customers' Needs

Help Desk Analysts should know as much about their customers as practical. For internal customers, this includes having access to information about customers' organizations and operating hours, specific configuration information about their physical location and hardware set up, and software configuration. This information is most useful if it is integrated into your problem-management system.

Additionally, experienced Help Desk analysts should know their customers' psychological needs. A particular customer service center, for example, may run several different applications. Losing several of those applications wouldn't make them happy, but it may not threaten their basic business. One particular application, however, might be absolutely critical...especially between noon and 5:00 p.m. on Fridays. Understanding these needs can make the difference in how customers perceive your Help Desk.

Even for Help Desks serving external customers, it is possible to build a database of customer information that can help the service process. This is often accomplished through the use of warranty or registration cards. Anything helps, since it is always pleasing to customers when the analyst recognizes them and knows something about their situation from the beginning.

Some form of caller identification can also help in this process. Caller ID can be useful. Help Desks can use simple techniques such as combining dedicated telephone service lines for selected areas with telephone displays to identify the caller's region. In more sophisticated systems, a voice response unit (VRU) can prompt the customer to enter a unique ID over the telephone before the call is transferred to an analyst; any unique identifier can accomplish this, such as a Social Security number, device number or personal identification number (PIN). Analysts can then be prompted with relevant information about customers before they have said a word. Skills-based routing can be used to direct calls to an analyst with specific training or expertise.

The Customer Liaison

Some internal Help Desks in large organizations designate individuals to represent the interests of large customer bases within or outside the IS organization. This person is usually the customer liaison. We can't overemphasize the importance of maintaining effective relationships with these individuals. In some cases, customer liaisons are active and visible, while in others they will go about their normal, day-to-day functions, only calling Help Desk management if they're having problems.

Whatever style the customer liaisons follow, it is critical you make yourself and your Help Desk visible to them. They often know about problems with your services that you don't. They may not seek you out to tell you – trying to be nice – but you need to be aware of these problems to resolve them before they boil over. A strong working relationship with these individuals can also help protect the Help Desk against undue criticism during problem times. In many cases, how well your Help Desk performs is less important than how these representatives feel about the job you're doing. Also, these representatives often will have your boss's ear.

The Art of Negotiation

Help Desk call handling presents many situations in which you need to negotiate with the customer. Negotiation involves recognizing the needs of the customer, comparing these needs with your organization's ability to deliver what is required, then reaching a compromise that satisfies both parties. This information can be used to develop service level agreements, which are discussed in more detail in Chapter 13.

When handling calls, you may encounter a customer making an unreasonable demand or expecting a response quicker than the priority of the problem warrants. Use open questions to determine the customer's actual need. You might find a hidden problem the Help Desk or the customer needs to address.

When you have assessed the situation and decided on a course of action, it's important to be direct and specific in your statements. With some customers, you'll need to be assertive. If the customer is still unwilling to accept the situation, refer the problem to a supervisor. At all times, you need to remain positive and service oriented.

How to Recognize and Manage Behavior

Every customer is different. Agents should learn to recognize these differences and adjust their behavior accordingly. This section addresses different techniques for dealing with difficult customers. While difficult customers present your staff with exceptional challenges, they represent opportunities to demonstrate skills, fix problems, and develop or rebuild good customer relationships.

To understand difficult customers you must first understand the three basic communication behaviors. These behaviors are passive, aggressive and assertive.

Passive Behavior

On the surface, passive people seem easy to work with. They usually appear agreeable and hide other feelings. However, they generally have a great deal of stress because they seldom get what they want; they let others walk all over them. Passive people usually remain passive for only so long. Often, they become adept at blocking or even sabotaging others' efforts without taking responsibility for their actions. Because they have not made their own desires or needs clear, negotiating with them is difficult. This often results in frustration and surprises for those dealing with them.

Passive customers can be difficult to recognize, since at first they appear so agreeable. If a customer's behavior strikes you as more timid or accommodating than the severity of their problem warrants, you may be dealing with a passive customer. The key to managing passive customers is attempting to draw them out by asking open-ended questions. Make sure you clarify the impact of the problem, since these customers may understate the level of severity. Double-check any agreements you make with these customers to ensure they agree with the resolution or planned action, and are not just being "nice."

Aggressive Behavior

Aggressive people are very capable of expressing their own feelings and needs, but do so in a way that violates the rights of others. Aggressive behaviors include blaming, threatening, humiliating and dominating. Aggressive people are difficult because they care nothing about the rights of others. They always seem to get their way, but also have a lot of stress because they are always involved in conflict.

Aggressive customers are easy to recognize by their bullying tactics. In dealing with this type of person, it's important not to react emotionally to his/her behavior. Don't become defiant or unhelpful or enter into a direct confrontation. And don't give in to the aggressive customer's unreasonable demands.

How do you deal with aggressive customers? First, actively acknowledge and empathize with their problems to cool down these people. Second, if you can satisfy their requests by normal processes, do it, regardless of their behavior. If not, explain what you can and can't do and why. Attempt to secure some sort of agreement through closed-ended questions. If the customer is still unsatisfied, refer the call to a supervisor before your patience becomes exhausted.

Assertive Behavior

Assertive people know and respect their own rights as well as the rights of others. Assertive behavior increases the chance of a compromise or satisfactory result without making others angry. No one's life is stress-free, but assertive people generally have less stress and find what stress they do have to be manageable.

Although assertive customers usually will be more demanding than passive customers, in the long run your agents will learn to appreciate their directness and willingness to compromise. Also, assertive customers always present the fewest unpleasant surprises to both analysts and Help Desk managers.

Managing Angry Customers

We all get angry from time to time, regardless of our basic communication style, and Help Desk analysts are often faced with customers who are intensely frustrated. At the start of the call, angry customers will always seem aggressive to the agent; as these customers cool off they will usually drop back into their normal style of communication. The following guidelines help agents deal with angry or frustrated callers.

Prepare yourself. Take an extra deep breath and be prepared to listen to your customer's angry words without taking them personally. Try to keep a pleasant attitude in your mind and in your voice.

Let your customer vent the anger. Don't interrupt, even if you know how to solve the problem. These customers aren't prepared to listen until they've finished "getting it off their chests."

Listen and take notes. Write down your customer's exact words as best you can.

Refer to your notes and paraphrase what the customer said to make sure you understand the situation. Be sure to communicate to the customer that you were listening. Use the customer's name frequently.

Empathize with the customer. Say something like, "I understand how this could be frustrating. We'll find a solution together." This preserves your customer's dignity and usually defuses the anger.

Ask, "What would you like for a solution?" If the request is workable, do it; if not, look for alternatives. Explain what can and can't be done and, if possible, offer options to the customer. This makes your customer an owner of the solution.

Get agreement. Verify your customer's understanding and acceptance of the solution.

Take care of yourself. After particularly stressful calls, it's important to take a few seconds to take a deep breath and let the physical effects of the stress wear off. Check yourself to make sure you've calmed down before taking another call. If necessary, ask for time away from the phone.

Tips for Building Customer Relationships

Admit when you don't know the answer to a customer's problem. It is far better to say, "I don't know, but I'll find out" than to pretend to know the answer and be unable to explain it.

If you give a customer an answer you later realize was wrong, contact the customer as soon as practical. The customer will be happier to learn the correct answer now, than encounter further problems later.

Avoid getting too casual with a customer, even if you have worked with the person many times. Don't eat or drink while on the telephone or use buzzwords or technical terminology that may be unfamiliar to the customer.

Be sure to acknowledge the importance of the problem to the customer. Paraphrase the nature of the problem as well as its importance to make sure you understand the situation. Never imply that a customer's problem is "no big deal."

If you need to follow up on a problem for a customer, return the call within an agreed-upon period of time. This is important even if you only let the customer know you're addressing the problem. If the customer does not answer the phone, leave a message stating the current status. If there is no way to leave a message, use whatever method is available.

Periodically review the problems or questions initiated by specific customers. If questions are repeatedly about the same software, you might suggest the customer take a class, or you might need to notify the software maintenance team if it involves a design problem. If the calls involve repetitive hardware problems, bring this to the attention of someone in hardware maintenance. The ability to track problems like this depends on two procedures: regularly reviewing problems and properly logging all calls.

Accentuate the Positive

Analysts' attitudes are key to Help Desk success. The staff's general morale and attitude will be reflected in how they treat their customers. Managers have more impact on this positive environment than they realize. The most important aspect is the manager's attitude. If a manager is calm, supportive, strongly oriented toward customer service and is a good listener, then the Help Desk personnel will ultimately reflect those qualities. A good rule of thumb is to ask the staff to treat each other the same way they are expected to treat customers. This goes for managers, too.

Managers also need to be sensitive to periods when Help Desk stress levels are particularly high. This is an opportunity to show real leadership by finding ways to relieve the pressure.

Ideas for promoting healthly attitudes:

1. Give a simple, public thank you for work well done
2. Recongnize special contributions
3. Provide free snacks or drinks
4. Host an after-hours dinner or party
5. Promote the best performers
6. Get special thanks from a senior manager in the company

Six ideas for promoting healthy attitudes at the Help Desk   Figure 5-2

Figure 5-2 presents some approaches for keeping attitudes healthy at your Help Desk. These approaches include giving a public thank-you for work well done, recognizing special contributions, providing free snacks or drinks, hosting an after-hours dinner or party, getting special acknowledgment from a senior manager in the company and promoting the best performers. [There are other possibilities. Be inventive: there are many ways that you can help relieve pressure or express your appreciation.]

Finally, humor is the greatest stress release for us all. You need to use it carefully, however, since ill-placed humor can easily offend. The safest and best-appreciated humor is to poke fun at oneself. This can be especially effective when senior managers are willing to allow harmless jokes at their own expense.

For a more thorough treatment on the topic of customer relationships, refer to Help Desk Institute's self-study course Customer Service Skills for Help Desk Professionals

Chapter 7

By Eugene Ball

Telephony

Telephony

Telephony is the science of converting sound into electrical signals, transmitting it within cables or via radio, and reconverting it back into sound. Broadly, the term refers to the telephone industry in general. In the support industry, the term applies specifically to the telephone systems we use to connect our customers with our Help Desk.

The following is a description of the four basic tools in the telephony chain.

PBX

Private branch exchange (PBX) is an in-house telephone switching system that interconnects telephone extensions to each other, as well as to the outside telephone network. PBX may include functions such as least-cost routing for outside calls, call forwarding, conference calling, and call accounting. Modern PBXs use all-digital methods for switching and may support both digital terminals and telephones, along with analog telephones. In some cases, the PBX is owned not by the corporate user, but by the local telephone company.

ACD

Automatic call distributor (ACD) is a computerized phone system that routes incoming telephone calls to the next available operator or agent. ACDs are the electronic heart of support centers, and they are

widely used by many departments of an organization. The ACD responds
to the caller with a voice menu and connects the call to an appropriate
individual.

IVR

Interactive voice response (IVR) is an automated telephone answering system that responds with a voice menu and allows the user to make
choices and enter information via the phone keypad or voice. IVR systems
are widely used in support centers as a front end for ACDs, to offload as
many calls as possible from costly human analysts. The system may also
integrate database access and fax response.

The IVR allows the caller to enter a single digit selection and enter
numeric data using the telephone keypad or by voice. The IVR can help
manage the queues by providing information to the customers in a queue,
for example the average wait time.

CTI

Computer-telephone integration (CTI) technology combines data
with voice systems in order to enhance telephone services. For inbound
calls, one example of CTI is automatic number identification (ANI), which
allows a caller's records to be retrieved from the database while the call is
routed to the appropriate party. For outbound calls, automatic telephone
dialing from an address list provides another example of CTI at work.

Each of the tools, PBX, ACD, and IVR, has well defined functions.

The PBX is the first in the line of these tools. The PBX handles the
basic functions of a business' telephone system, such as call forwarding,
conference calling, least-cost routing for outside calls, and basic call
accounting, where basic means basic and not very useful in the management
of your Help Desk. If your only telephony tool is a PBX, then the customer
may be routed to a phone that is not busy where they may get
  • Connected with an analyst,
  • Routed to the next free analyst after a predefined number
    of rings,
  • A busy signal, or
  • Directed to voice mail.
Almost all Help Desks work with a PBX either as part of the PBX
owned by their company or by the telephone provider.

The ACD is the first telephony tool added when a Help Desk is trying to improve customer service or productivity. First remember that not all ACDs are created equal. The ACD may allow the Help Desk management to define queues. The ACD allows the customer phone key input to voice questions or instructions such as:

- Push 1 if you are a new customer,
- Push 2 if you need your password reset,
- Etc.

Each of these selections moves the customer into different queues, which allows the Help Desk to handle each of these queues differently.

In addition to the voice directions and queues, the ACD can provide the Help Desk management with many important statistics that are not provided by the PBX such as:
- Average hold time,
- Average speed to answer,
- Longest hold time,
- Number of inbound calls per interval,
- Number of abandons per interval,
- Average talk time per analysts,
- Amount of time an analyst is available to receive calls,
- Average wrap-up time per analysts,
- Etc.

These types of statistics when used properly are valuable tools for Help Desk management as they strive to improve the level of service staff productivity.

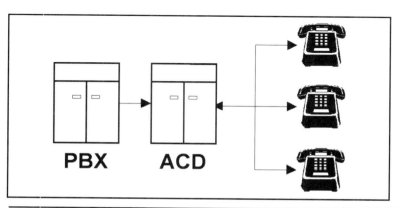

Illustrates the location of the ACD in the telephony configuration.   Figure 1

After the ACD has been installed into the telephony system, the next tool added is the IVR. While the ACD by itself allows callers to make only single-digit selections using the telephone keypad, the IVR further enables callers to enter multi-digit numeric data using the telephone keypad. A new addition to the IVR is the ability to use speech-recognition technology. Speech recognition has added functionality such as the ability to recognize a user ID that contains alpha characters. Speech-recognition technology has made major advances in the last several years.

Increased Information Output

The IVR can be used to provide just-in-time education without losing the caller's place in the queue. Short tips can be provided and the type of tips can be related to the type of queue each caller is in. If the customer's place is kept in the queue, then the customer will be more inclined to listen and learn. The IVR can further manage queues by providing information about average wait time. For those callers experiencing long wait times, the IVR can offer alternatives. For example, an on-hold message can suggest to callers that they use the IVR to get technical assistance. The system can interact with callers to learn about their problems and recommend likely solutions from a database. The IVR can even be used in conjunction with a fax server to send requested information. The fax can be generated based on customers' responses to questions presented by the IVR.

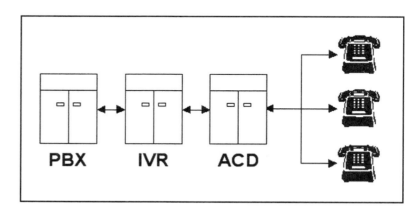

Figure 2   Illustrates the location of VRU application in the telephony implementation.

The telephony framework can be completed by adding CTI to the mix. CTI is the merging of computer and telephony hardware and software technologies to provide high-tech, user-friendly services. A simplistic explanation is that a CTI system takes information from the telephone system—be it PBX, ACD and/or IVR systems—and uses that information to interact with other computers.

A common CTI feature is the screen-pop. When a customer calls the Help Desk, the telephone system delivers the automatic number identification (ANI) or caller's telephone number to the CTI system. The CTI system displays the ANI plus information about the caller on the designated analyst's computer screen. The additional data is retrieved via the CTI system from an in-house database as the caller and the analyst are connected.

One problem with the above CTI application example is the phone number delivered to the recipient may not be helpful; for example, all phone calls coming from another company's PBX could have the same ANI or the customer may be calling from a phone that is not connected with the customer information in the database. In such cases, the correct customer data would not be delivered to the analyst. If these or similar examples happen often, it would be useful to place an IVR between the PBX and CTI to gather more information from the caller, such as the caller's personal ID (PID) number.

A variation of the screen-pop is the use of an IVR to gather more information from the customer, such as the customer's ID number. With the customer's ID number, the system can provide better results when retrieving data from the RMS database.

Using the ACD and IVR to gather information from the customer, it is possible to automate many time-consuming tasks, such as status information about an open problem. In this implementation, the ACD moves the customer to a queue for open-problem status. The IVR prompts the customer for the open-problem (RMS) number (here, voice-to-text technology can be used). The IVR passes this information to the CTI application, which retrieves predetermined information from the RMS ticket, such as the ticket status, date and time of the last update, and the text of the last update. Now the CTI application passes the retrieved data back to the IVR, and the IVR, using text-to-voice technology, reads the information to the customer.

Another task that can be automated is password resets. Again, the ACD moves the customer to a queue for password resets. The IVR prompts the customer for the necessary information, such as customer ID or name, system for which the password is needed and a PID. The IVR passes the information to the CTI application. The CTI application then communicates with software that can reset the password. That software can also send the new password back to the IVR through the CTI application, and the IVR can read the new password to the customer. However, security concerns may require the IVR to call the customer to provide the password (text-to-voice technology) or may require the CTI application to e-mail the password to the customer.

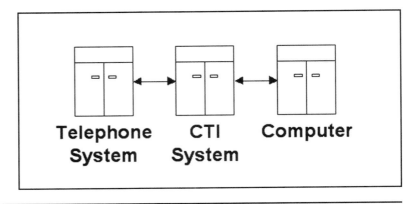

Figure 3   Illustrates the location of the CTI application in the telephony configuration.

Summary

Until recently, the communication between tools in the telephony chain and the analyst's phone has used basic analog or digital telephone communication. Now the use of voice-over IP (VoIP) is growing. The use of an IP network has introduced several significant changes. The first is that more than one application (PBX, ACD, IVR and CTI) can be supported by a single piece of hardware. In addition, the single piece of hardware can also support voice mail, e-mail and Web interface. Such a box with multiple applications offers several benefits, such as:
- Reducing the overall hardware cost
- Productivity gains by allowing the analyst to use a single portal for all types of communication with the customer

• Cost savings driven by flexibility
• Ease of management

The one down-side to the use of multiple telephony application hardware is reliability. When each PBX, ACD, IVR and CTI application resided on its own hardware server, the expected up time was better than 99 percent because the hardware components were selected and tested for the single application. By placing several applications on a single piece of hardware, the likelihood of software conflicts and system failures increases.

Chapter 8

By Anna Guy

Call Handling Techniques

How can you quickly and accurately diagnose and resolve problems? This chapter presents techniques for gathering complete information regarding your customers' problems. This will better prepare you for prioritizing these problems, maintaining ownership after they've been assigned, and following up on their resolution whenever necessary.

Initial Problem Diagnosis

The Help Desk analyst typically bases the initial diagnosis on problem symptoms and reports the diagnosis in the form of predefined problem-classification codes.

Information to identify with problem classification codes:

1. Problem type key words
2. Affected application
3. Network and mainframe
4. Transaction
5. Error codes/messages
6. Component key item
7. Region transaction
8. Customer identification and location
9. Priority/severity level
10. Category and cause
11. Tracking numbers

Information to identify with problem classification codes   Figure 7-1

Figure 7-1 details information Help Desks often identify with problem-classification codes. Some of these codes include problem-type keywords, the affected application, network or mainframe, customer information, priority, error codes, cause and job number.

It's important that Help Desk analysts and all Help Desk support partners understand these code types and acceptable values. In addition to the predefined codes, most systems have a free-form narrative area where you can document relevant information for later problem analysis.

Many Help Desks handle calls in a question-and answer-format, guiding the customer to supply the information necessary for problem resolution or assignment. Some Help Desk analysts review checklists with customers and can diagnose and resolve most procedural problems. Help Desks develop standard checklists by problem type, application and equipment.

Help Desks have reported good results from handling the beginning portion of each call as an open-ended question, allowing the customer to talk freely. Agents then ask closed-ended questions to gain specific information. Open-ended questions at the start of calls provide customers the opportunity to vent any frustrations and express their thought about the problems and possible resolutions. You can then further clarify customers' problems by paraphrasing or repeating what you understand the problem to be.

The appropriate method for initial problem diagnosis is determined by the knowledge or skill level of the Help Desk agent. To aid in the initial diagnosis, ask the customer about any error codes or messages displayed. One effective technique for gathering information at this stage is to explain to customers the relevance of the information requested. This helps customers become more knowledgeable and better use the Help Desk's services in the future.

Help Desks can enhance initial diagnosis by using an automated system to provide online access to problem history. Some systems have problem files containing the number of problems that have occurred by device, by location and in total for the previous week. If multiple occurrences of problems by device or location develop, the Help Desk can consider each problem and alert personnel to the need for permanent resolution.

Effective Help Desk systems provide historical, attached-to-device (configuration), network availability and change information as the analyst records the problem.

Questions to Consider

We've developed some questions for you to consider when evaluating your Help Desk's diagnostic techniques:

- What information is available to your analysts from your system? Do you have the customer's hardware configuration? Their problem history?
- Do your analysts have current information from a change-management system? Have the programs or hardware recently been changed? Has the data center had any change in its operating environment?
- What are the recognizable symptoms of the problem? Are others in the caller's area affected by the problem? Are there any systemwide problems? Is there any reference material indicating possible solutions based on known symptoms?
- Is there a code associated with the problem? Are there any messages displayed associated with a particular application or a particular software package?
- Do you have remote-control software, or some ability to simulate the customer's workstation, to help your analysts diagnose and analyze the problem? Has the program been updated with current information and methods of detecting known problems?
- Is there anything different about the input to the customer's system? Is the volume of data higher than in the past?

Setting Priorities

One of the measures of a good manager is the ability to distinguish the important from the urgent. And just because something is urgent does not necessarily mean you should work on it at once. The same is true of a good problem-management system and the processes that run it. Prioritizing action items ensures your Help Desk uses its resources in the most effective manner.

Sample method of qualifying severity codes:

Level	Definition	Expected Response
Severity 1	Production is down for a large number of customers and work cannot continue until the problem is fixed	All parties including vendors are expected to work continuously (including nights and weekends) until the problem is resolved
Severity 2	Tremendous inconvenience to customers – but a temporary circumvention, or "work-around" is in place	Work is expected to continue on a workday basis until a more permanent solution is in place
Severity 3	Mild inconvenience – a smaller customer base or a milder problem	Resolution is worked into a planned project list and scheduled
Severity 4	More minor still	Resolution can be deferred until time allows, but eventually should be fixed
Severity 5	Trivial	Deferred indefinitely unless something causes the perception of its importance to change, at which time the Help Desk will raise the severity level

---

Figure 7-2   A sample method of qualifying severity codes

One method of setting a priority is to determine the number of impacted customers and establish whether the customers can work around the problem. Many organizations set priorities based on the estimated dollar impact and the number of customers affected. Today, it's common for the customer to help establish ground rules for setting priorities. Then, during an actual problem, the customer can assist the Help Desk analyst in appropriately defining the problem's priority.

You can assign priority levels to problems. Figure 7-2 shows one system, originally developed by IBM. This system uses a severity numbering system of 1 through 5, 1 being the most severe. In this system, documentation changes often fall into the severity 3 category.

Example of expected arrival times of priority levels:

Priority	Expected arrival
Priority level 1	Immediately
Priority level 2	Two hours
Priority level 3	Next day
Priority level 4	Three days
Priority level 5	No special trip – next visit

An example of expected arrival times of five priority levels   Figure 7-3

Figure 7-3 presents an approach for setting priorities by defining time limits for the arrival of a response team. This approach is particularly useful for problems requiring onsite response such as hardware problems at the customer site. You can explain these time limits to customers so they can help set the proper priorities.

While you can set expectations for the response to a problem and the effort to resolve it, you can't determine the actual time-to-resolution in advance. No one knows how difficult or time consuming any one problem will be.

Limit the number of problems that are assigned a high priority to a practical minimum, since your Help Desk can only work on a given number of problems at once. Typically, the Help Desk manager needs to approve a high-priority designation.

One technique for evaluating your Help Desk could be determining whether it uses high priorities too often; this indicates an over-reaction to the severity of problems.

Call Ownership

When you escalate a call to another area, who is responsible for resolving the problem? Most organizations prefer to keep the ownership at the Help Desk. Doing so provides a single point of contact for the customer, which provides consistency in determining if a problem is really resolved. This procedure also serves as reinforcement for those customers who call the Help Desk for support, and discourages them from calling your support partners directly.

Call Follow-up

It may not be possible for your Help Desk to follow up on every problem it handles to ensure the customer is satisfied. When considering which problems to follow up on, consider the following points:

- Priority-one problems should come first. Always follow up on these incidents to verify that the problem was resolved to the customer's satisfaction.
- If customers are irritated, you may not feel like talking to them again. However, it is important to follow up. Customers will probably be surprised to hear back from the Help Desk and your concern may encourage a more pleasant association in the future.
- Follow up with repeat callers to be sure they didn't call back simply out of frustration. This follow-up enhances their perception of the Help Desk and encourages these customers to call in the future.
- Any problem assigned to another area is also a likely candidate for a follow-up call. The assignee should deal with the Help Desk to close the problem, but customers should have the opportunity to verify that the problem has been resolved to their satisfaction.
- Also follow up on problems you resolved on first contact that had a high-dollar impact or affected a large number of customers.

If the customer does not agree that the problem has been resolved, then you may need to reopen the problem record, document the status of the problem from the customer's current point of view and make another attempt to resolve the problem.

Chapter 9

By Anna Guy

Problem Assignment and Resolution

Your Help Desk should strive to solve as many calls as possible on first contact. In cases where you don't have the resources to solve the problem, your Help Desk needs to assign the problem to another area. The organization or individual receiving the assignment is called the assignee. Be sure to keep some measurements on the percentage of calls that the Help Desk must assign to someone else; a high number may indicate insufficient Help Desk training.

We'll be using three key terms throughout this chapter: assignment, escalation and notification. You may find that Help Desks define these terms differently or use them interchangeably. However, your organization needs to use these terms consistently throughout your Help Desk operations. We've defined these terms in the following paragraphs.

Assignment: This process involves passing lead resolution responsibility from the Help Desk to another support partner in accordance with preapproved, documented procedures for this type of problem.

Escalation: In the escalation process, the Help Desk analyst or manager notifies senior staff members of all appropriate support partners so they are aware of the situation and can apply appropriate resources to resolve the problem.

Notification: This process involves communicating the nature and severity of the problem to customer representatives so they may take steps to mitigate the impact to their organizations.

In the pages that follow, we'll discuss the assignment, escalation and notification processes in detail so you can implement these processes at your Help Desk to more quickly and accurately resolve your customers' problems.

Assignment Process

Problem assignment at the Help Desk generally is made by routing the problem to one of its support partners, based on documented procedures. These procedures identify support coverage based on the type of problem, time of day, day of week, problem priority and escalation status.

Your Help Desk needs to have an understanding with the support partner assigned to the incident that they will handle problems according to the escalation procedures and service-level agreements of the Help Desk.

Even when you assign a problem, the Help Desk continues to own it, from the customer's point of view. The Help Desk must track the progress of the support partner that is now driving problem resolution.

.

Determining Severity Codes

Escalate problems to management based on the initial severity and after a specified period passes. The problem severity code and application area determine how and to whom the problem is escalated. Some firms use a problem coordinator or network availability manager to establish severity codes. Others route problems by classification code to the head of the specific problem area and establish the severity codes at that level. Although in the past the Help Desk typically set the severity code when a problem was reported, more firms now work with customers in advance to define severity codes based on well-defined problem types and customer impact.

Managing the Data

The data your Help Desk supplies to an assigned support partner depends on the system you use. Generally, the support partner should have the information initially reported to the Help Desk, including the priority level.

Direct contact between the support and the customer should be the exception rather than the rule. Over time, such contact may result in the customer directly calling these technical support personnel. At many Help Desks, analysts call the customers and conference-in the support partner. This also helps keep the Help Desk current on the problem status. In some cases, support partners may need to contact the caller directly, but they should not leave their name or telephone number.

How to Provide Data to the Support Partner

Your Help Desk may use an automated problem-handling system as the primary source for providing problem information to the support partner. The problem report is routed in the system and can be accessed by the support partner as well as Help Desk personnel. The system can supply a date/time stamp to document when a problem was first reported. For priority problems, the Help Desk will likely contact the support partner to ensure it received the information and clearly understands the facts and severity.

Some organizations use call log sheets or trouble tickets to communicate problem assignment information. Such forms also generally allow the support partner to document the resolution.

Your Help Desk should establish procedures to ensure the support partner is provided with all necessary information. One method is to meet with each department and determine what information is critical to resolving problems related to its area. The Help Desk uses this information to customize or create subscreens in the problem-management system to capture the needed information for specific problem types.

Some companies use display bulletin boards to alert the Help Desk staff of current outstanding problems. This is necessary to prevent multiple assignments. When the Help Desk receives a call for an already-reported problem, agents can reference the original record of the problem and add new information to the log. This way, agents don't assign the problem or manage it as new.

Data Elements to Track

Help Desks maintain numerous tools and techniques to record, assign, resolve, track, report and manage problems. Help Desks use this data to analyze problem histories, monitor open problems, create reports, support meetings and monitor vendors.

Elements you can use when tracking problems:

1. Problem number
2. Problem type/subtype
3. Component
4. Workstation
5. Node
6. Transactions
7. Error code
8. Application
9. Job number
10. Step number
11. Program name
12. Region
13. Network address
14. Serial number
15. Product
16. Problem symptom
17. Problem classification
18. Problem category
19. Cause code
20. Problem priority
21. Reported by/reported to
22. Location
23. Phone number

24. Assigned to (multiple)
25. Time/date fields
   -Reported
   -Occurred
   -Assigned (multiple)
   -Assignee received (multiple)
   -Vendor called
   -Vendor opened
   -Vendor closed
   -Resolved (multiple)
   -Closed
26. Actions taken
27. Narrative ("search on text")
28. Frequency of occurrence
29. Reference to other related problems

Figure 8-1   Elements you can use when tracking problems

Figure 8-1 presents a sample list of data elements Help Desks track. Agents gather much of this information during problem documentation.

Although several organizations maintain problem histories from day one, companies with integrated problem-history information typically limit the amount of online problem history in order to enhance response time. An average duration for maintaining online problem history is six to 12 months; after that, the Help Desk archives the data to offline files. For long-term tracking, agents can later process this data in batch mode or temporarily restore it to online storage.

Be sure to consider security concerns such as who should be allowed to view, input or update problem-tracking data elements. This is especially true for authorization to close problems and for archiving or deleting data.

Assignment Techniques

Assignment techniques usually depend on the problem-classification codes and problem severity. Many Help Desks have a list of first, second and third persons to contact for a specific category. The reference list may include office phone numbers, e-mail addresses, home phones, pager numbers and car phone numbers. You can automate this reference assignment list or print it. Keeping the list up to date and maintaining easy access to this list is vital.

Assignment techniques vary by organization and priority of the problem. A few assignment techniques include using primary and backup support staff, holding daily meetings, escalating unresolved problems and conducting management reviews.

Primary and Backup Support Staff

Many companies use a cross-reference list to assign problems to support groups during regular business hours. The list is kept online by application and is often supplemented by a daily on-call list. After hours, companies may supply on-call staff with pagers and list these staff members by individual or by application.

Daily Meetings

Assignment procedures typically include daily morning meetings. The Help Desk manager reviews open problems with the staff and other managers and ensures all responsible parties receive the information they need to resolve the problems. Help Desks can also assign problems by conference calls or teleconference. For example, the Help Desk of a large financial concern manages open problems with remote sites by conducting daily video conferences.

Escalating Unsolved Problems

The relationship of assigned problems to escalation varies from organization to organization. Figure 8-2 presents an example of a priority escalation procedure.

Sample priority escalation procedure:

	Initial priority level	Time unresolved	Escalated to priority level
Problem #1	2	one day	1
Problem #2	3	three days	2

Figure 8-2   Sample priority escalation procedure

Usually, assignment to a second-level support group does not require escalation. If a problem requires assignment to third-level support, or if a problem has remained unsolved beyond a specified period—perhaps a full day—then the Help Desk will escalate that problem. The degree of escalation is based on the problem's effect on the company's ability to do business, as well as the length of time since the problem occurred.

Some organizations escalate open problems first to the Help Desk manager and, later, involve upper-level staff and executive managers if the problem continues. The number of escalations that occur until the problem reaches top management depends on the type of problem. No matter how many people become involved, the Help Desk must stay aware of all escalated problems and get regular updates on its current status. This is critical for the Help Desk's credibility and the manager's credibility.

Escalating the priority of a problem is ordinarily a management decision. It may involve a higher level of management, depending on the severity level or the number of times the Help Desk has had to escalate the problem.

Management Review

At higher levels of management, such as vice presidents, problem escalation is informational in nature. This is often called notification, since these managers usually aren't able to resolve problems but may need to know their status. A strictly followed escalation and notification policy, with no informal handoffs, is critical to problem management.

Importance of Help Desk Ownership

Never tell customers to call another support partner directly. This can result in a host of problems for both the Help Desk and its customers.

If customers call other areas for support, it may negatively affect the productivity of the customers and the support partner. Customers may not be able to reach anyone in that area, they may misstate the symptoms of the problem or the Help Desk may have misinterpreted the symptoms, in which case the problem may require a different support partner.

Additionally, if a support partner resolves a problem presented to them directly, they may not properly document the information and it may be lost; if other Help Desk customers are experiencing the same problem it may be assigned to another support partner, making the direct contact unnecessary.

When customers go directly to other areas for support, the Help Desk may not know if or when the problem is resolved, and customers could end up getting the runaround.

Customer Notification

When major system or application problems occur, the Help Desk can play a crucial role in minimizing the impact on its customers, even though it is usually beyond the ability of the Help Desk to resolve those problems directly.

Customer notification involves informing the customer community of major system problems so customers know the Help Desk and appropriate support groups are aware of the problem and will provide updates on its status.

Note that we distinguish notification from escalation. The people we notify—our customers—have a need to be aware of a problem but are not necessarily expected to have a role in resolving it.

Purpose of Notification

Customer notification can have a major, positive impact on customer productivity and satisfaction, because it alerts customers to these incidents and keeps them informed. Notification can also positively impact the Help Desk's productivity by preventing repeat phone calls and interruptions, allowing agents to concentrate on the problem at hand.

Using various techniques, the Help Desk can notify the impacted customer groups of information, such as the expected duration of an outage, status updates and outage recovery.

Customer notification contributes to customer productivity and satisfaction by letting customers know a problem is a general problem not associated with their individual systems. It prevents downtime when analysts can instruct customers on ways to work around the problem. Notification also gets customers back to work as quickly as possible, once the outage problem is resolved, which assures the customer community that the Help Desk is aware of the importance of their work.

Notification Techniques

Many Help Desks create matrices indicating the segments of a customer population that are impacted by the failure of particular applications, particular systems, or even single hardware components. This enables the Help Desk to provide specific information and helps analysts communicate the severity of a problem to the appropriate support partners.

Telephone Messages:

Use system-wide voice mail or call customer centers or departments and give the message to a point person.

Digital Recorders:

Place notification message on an auto attendant, so incoming callers hear the message before they reach an analyst. In many instances, this is all they need to know and they terminate the call.

Electronic Display Boards:

This tool can be helpful and cost effective for large customer sites in critical areas such as senior management headquarters or central data centers.

Electronic Mail:

This tool is helpful when notifying all your customers or providing specific information to specific customers.

Pagers:

Help Desks usually only use pagers to notify senior managers of problems rather than customers.

Problem Resolution

Help Desk resolution is defined as achieving a satisfactory result for the customer without assigning the call to another support partner.

Depending upon the nature of the calls, the staff resources available, and the systems and information in use, Help Desks can resolve between 20 to 98% of all calls. Many mature Help Desks consistently resolve 80 to 90% of incoming calls. In fact, knowledgeable agents can

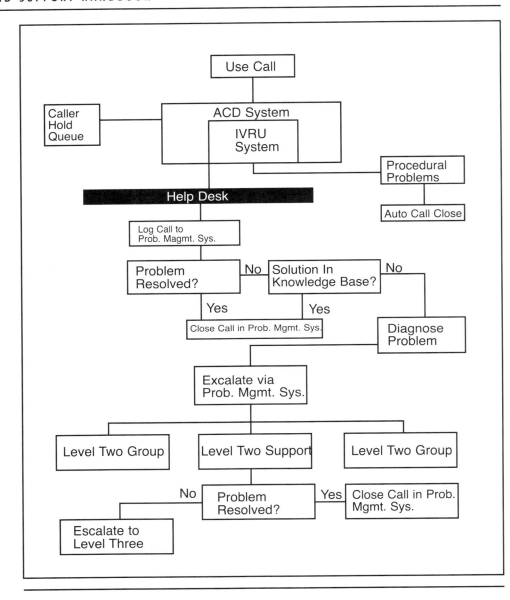

Figure 8-3   Illustrates the problem resolution at a typical
             Help Desk

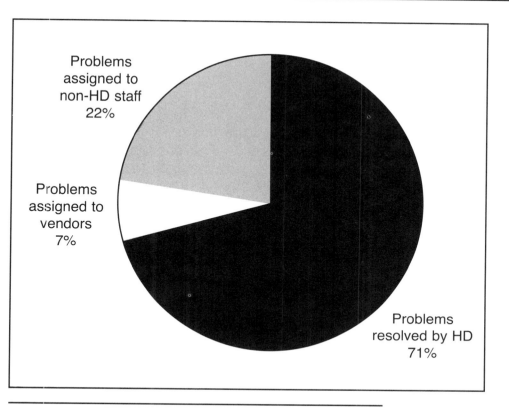

Problems
assigned to
non-HD staff
22%

Problems
assigned to
vendors
7%

Problems
resolved by HD
71%

Chart from Help Desk Institute's 1993 Help Desk
Practices Survey showing the percentage of problems
solved by the Help Desk

Figure 8-4

resolve many problems during the initial call based on the information
they receive and their experience.

Access to problem history and configuration data enhances the
Help Desk's ability to resolve problems when receiving calls. Searching
problem history in an automated system using problem types and keywords can help you resolve problems. Formalized shift turnover procedures also help gather and disburse recent resolution information, as well
as information on outstanding problems.

When you can't resolve problems during the initial call, offer customers several suggestions for working around the problem, and give them an estimate of the time it might take to resolve the problem and when to expect a call back.

When you need specialists' help to resolve problems and they are not immediately available, customers often must wait for a return call. Therefore, you need to record the details of the problem for the person assigned to the situation. Recording this information reduces the details the customer will need to repeat to the specialist.

Closing Problems

Does your Help Desk resolve and close problems without adequately documenting the cause? Many organizations address this issue by making problem resolution and problem closing separate steps.

In many Help Desks, the agent who resolves the problem is not the same person who closes the problem. For escalated problems, the support partner—the person who resolves the problem—should not be the person who closes the problem in the system. The Help Desk should follow up and close the problem with the customer's approval. Closing problems separately from resolution of problems ensures only Help Desk staff can record the problem's cause and its resolution.

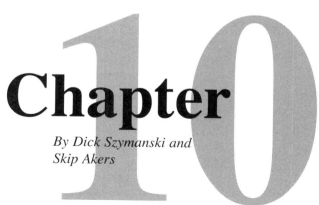

Chapter 10

*By Dick Szymanski and
Skip Akers*

Why and How to Measure

Organizational efficiencies usually can be seen through the kind of data that is tracked and measured. By keeping in touch with the market, the firm that treats such feedback as an opportunity will grow and thrive. Similarly, the information services organization that harnesses the vast wealth of customer input regarding its tools, systems and services intended to increase customer productivity (and, incidentally, make the company more profitable) will prosper.

As the central point of contact with both the enterprise community and the myriad operations that make the information services organization work, Help Desk personnel are in a position to understand not only the significance of the metrics, but also the emotional impact customers feel when information systems are interrupted. Tracking and analyzing data at the Help Desk in no way detracts from management's responsibility to manage. Actually, it is through analysis that data is transformed into usable information with which management can make informed decisions.

In this chapter, we will discuss why it is important to use the Help Desk to measure operational data and how measuring can be accomplished in a way that has a positive impact.

Why Measure?

Before the information services organization (or product development/delivery group) begins to develop a measuring process, it is important to define why this activity is needed. The most basic and vital reason to measure is to better manage the organization and the resources allocated to it, in order to make our business enterprises more productive and profitable. ("You cannot manage what you cannot measure.") Additionally, it is logical that any measurement system should start at the Help Desk. Once this is done, the process should be expanded to cover the rest of the organization.

Why start with the Help Desk? Because a reporting system is only as good as the data it collects. The organization should take the time to ensure it is collecting the types of data necessary to help meet its goals and objectives. Certainly there are other ways to compartmentalize these areas of strategic impact; by their nature, there is significant overlap and in some cases not all apply to every enterprise. The important issue is not the sanctity of these particular strategic goals, but that our measurements are driven by the goals and objectives of the information services organization.

How To Measure?
Indeed this topic is two-fold: what to measure and how to analyze what is being measured. Properly collecting and even knowing the best and most complete data is pointless until something useful is done with it. Somewhere in the strategic planning process, organizations must make decisions about what they hope to achieve. To accomplish these specific objectives, certain key elements of the operations performed by the organization need to be collected, measured and analyzed.

It might be helpful to think of measuring and analyzing as a continuum. The most elemental point-for-point data collection describes the moment-for-moment or event-by-event gathering of raw data. An incident, its duration and everything about it that is worth knowing should be measured.

What To Measure?
Every organization can collect an infinite amount of data related to its support operations. The problem is determining the right types of data to collect and analyze. Too often an organization builds a data collection system without giving thought to why it is necessary.

First, Help Desks and support centers must create data repositories that are driven by the critical/key factors that determine success or failure. These correlations (ratios, rates, averages and distributions), in turn, must be driven by the strategy that drives the organization as a whole. The following table lists just a few of the data points to consider. Each organization must determine on its own what information is vital to its operation, and the impact related to not measuring these elements.

Strategic Objective	Correlations (Ratio / Rate / Average	Point for Point Data Elements
Improving System Effectiveness Reliability	Incident Volume Averages	Number of Incidents
Improving System Effectiveness Reliability	Repeat Incidents Percentages	Repeat Incident
Improving System Effectiveness Reliability	Failure Rates	Incident Product/Feature "Failed"
Increasing Customer Satisfaction	Speed of Answer Averages Wait (Hold, Queue) Time Averages	Time to Answer Incident
Increasing Customer Satisfaction	Abandon Rates	Abandoned Incidents
Increasing Customer Satisfaction	Complaints Percentages	Complaints
Increasing Customer Satisfaction	Service Level Compliance Ratios	Feature or Customer Service Level Target
Increasing Customer Satisfaction	Wrap Time Averages	Incident Wrap Time
Increasing Process Efficiencies	Response Time Averages	Response Time
Increasing Process Efficiencies	Agent Availability Rates	Staff Agent Availability
Increasing Process Efficiencies	Average Resolution Rates	Resolution Times
Increasing Process Efficiencies	Re-opened Incidents Percentages	Re-opened Incident
Increasing Process Efficiencies	Handle/Work Time Averages	Incident Handling/ Work Duration

Increasing Process Efficiencies	Incident Length Averages	Incident Length of time
Increasing Staff Satisfaction	Absentee Rates	Staff Agent Absence
Increasing Staff Satisfaction	Agent Turnover Rates	Staff Agent Departure
Reducing Cost	Self Registration Percentage	Incident Registration Method
Reducing Cost Method/Source	Self Resolution Percentage First Level Resolution Percentage	Incident Resolution
Reducing Cost	"Cost" per Incident Ratio	Labor, material, expense and/or overhead allocation used
Increasing Revenue and Profit	Incident Revenue	Revenue per Contact

Both the Help Desk (or support center) and the information services organization (or product development/delivery) must commit resources to accomplish accurate measurement. The systems and technology used and the support analyst's time invested (processes) in the operational support of the customer must be built with the recognition of the potential strategic value of the information that is produced during a support transaction.

For example:
- the product/feature/service that is not functioning,
- the triggers that accompany the problem,
- the amount of time out of service (and the nature of who was affected by it),
- the accurate fix to the problem (and whether or not it is permanent or temporary),
- the amount (and type) of effort to fix the problem.

These are all data points that act as a summary of many transactions. When properly analyzed, these summations can lead to increasing process efficiencies, improving system effectiveness/reliability, increasing customer or staff satisfaction, reducing cost, and/or increasing revenue and profit.

If our call-tracking systems are not designed to handle and promote collecting the right data and/or our analysts don't believe in the importance of capturing this data before they move to their next crisis, there will be little to analyze.

How to Analyze

Simply collecting data does not affect an organization's ability to compete or make a profit. However, an analysis of this data could provide management with an arsenal of information from which decisions that affect profitability can be made.

Information services organizations (or the product development/delivery group) need to commit, *along with* the Help Desk (or support center), separate resources for analyzing and interpreting the information. This will...

- allow the Help Desk/support center to continue providing effective real-time responses;
- shield the information services organization (or product development/delivery) from the day-to-day crises; and
- increase MUTUAL awareness of the issues that are germane to big wins

Trend Analysis

To make use of critical success factor data, there should always be an established point of reference. Statistically, this is often referred to as a baseline. A baseline allows for comparison between the current measurement (whatever it may be measuring) and a previous point in time for that exact same measurement. Note that using correlations allows for "apples to apples" comparison. It is of no use to compare this period's raw data (incident volumes, costs, hold times, whatever) to another without normalizing the comparison (same time period and other characteristics.) A measurement significantly (statistically) greater or worse than before is an indication of a movement in a positive or negative direction.

The exact same measurement recurring over a longer period of time (weekly, monthly, yearly) allows for trend analysis. However, caution should be exercised when analyzing isolated data points. Proper conclusions can usually be made only through comparison data. For example:

A severely steep, upward trend in the number of complaints

received during the holiday season may not be cause for alarm if a company specializes in toy sales. This is especially true if a comparison to previous years' data reveals the same trend. Better yet, the numbers follow an already accepted baseline, which could possibly indicate that no further action is currently required.

However, if management sought to reduce the number of complaints, a special study targeting this particular trend could be initiated. Organizations that operate on a philosophy of incremental process improvement should focus on no more than one or two major trends at a time.

Effective Reporting

Effective reporting begins by tracking easily measured statistics. These statistics could include total number of calls opened, closed and outstanding; calls by problem type; average response time; and network availability.

Your Help Desk can begin by tracking an area that can be easily measured on a monthly basis, then documenting ideas to improve the area. This sets a successful precedent, reduces the fear of tracking statistics and paves the way for more specific reporting, such as by individual staff member and by application areas.

The next step in reporting involves clearly presenting the information. You can improve problem analysis by showing percentages by categories, such as total calls by problem type, unit (e.g., application), and customer or department. Use these percentages to produce memos, graphs, pie charts and other easy-to-read documents. Keep in mind that you want to provide quick, concise overviews.

By tracking and comparing these trends to a baseline, organizations can ensure they have an accurate picture of their current position.

On the positive side, tracking trends will alert management to possible problems that may need resolution. Conversely, trends do not provide enough information to determine the actual cause. They simply highlight an area to management that may require a closer study.

Causal Analysis

After trending reports are produced, it is time to make comparisons to existing data to determine if they are within the already established baselines. If so, then no other action is required except, perhaps, offering praise to the departments or individuals doing a great job.

However, if there is a significant downward movement in a particular area, a study must be undertaken to determine the actual or probable cause. This study is commonly referred to as root-cause analysis or causal analysis.

Because causal analysis can be a very complex issue, for this handbook we will take a simplistic, yet powerful, approach. In its most basic form, the reason for a problem or incident can be attributed to either Special Cause or Common Cause.

Special Cause is normally attributed to a group of isolated occurrences: unrelated incidents that are not likely to reoccur under normal circumstances. However, incidents that were originally classified a Special Cause can later be redesignated as Common Cause if certain systemic elements appear to be connected.

If, through investigation, it is determined that the cause of an event or occurrence was due to Special Cause, once resolution is achieved to the satisfaction of the customer, no further action is required. An example of Special Cause could be a power outage due to an electrical storm. Once power is restored and the customers are satisfied, unless there are repeated outages, it is assumed that the problem was resolved.

Common Cause, on the other hand, is systemic in nature. Common causes of events or problems will usually point to one or more major factors. Answering the question associated with these factors will point to the probable cause and suggest a resolution.

- **Process Weakness** – Does a process actually exist to handle the situation at hand? Is there a written process to follow? Is the process adequate for the expected outcome? Are there holes or gaps in the process that need to be filled?
- **Process Discipline** –Are the people or the department assigned to perform the function following the process? Are they aware of its existence?
- **Training** – Is training required to perform the task? Is training available, if required? Is the process assigned to the right department or individual capable of performing the tasks?

Summary

Measuring and analyzing the data collected by an organization can have a profound effect on the levels of success achieved. Companies that take an active interest in reaching expected outcomes would find that analysis is the key to reaching objectives and ultimately increasing profit.

This is WHY You Measure!

With the information provided, you should also understand how the process works. Applying the principles and techniques presented here will allow organizations to maximize the effective use of data collected. Analysis will also make the job of problem resolution a whole lot easier.

Chapter 11

By Chris Farver, Rick Joslin and Char LaBounty

The Evolution of Knowledge Management

In the early ninties, the term "expert systems" was the latest buzz-word and many of the major vendors in the marketplace at that time were jumping on the bandwagon. At that time early adopters focused on just the "technology" and not the cultural changes necessary to effectively turn expert systems into a viable working solution for their organizations. Today, expert systems as a technology have evolved as just one small aspect of a much broader set of initiatives falling under the term knowledge management.

Early success in knowledge management in the support center was a result of prepackaged knowledge bases entering the market in 1994. Support centers could purchase knowledge bases on third-party applications like Microsoft Windows, Microsoft Office and Novell Netware. Support centers supported more than generic applications; they supported proprietary applications and custom configurations, and they needed knowledge management to be able to add to these knowledge bases.

Knowledge management in its most simplistic term is the concept of finding, organizing and managing the knowledge of the people within an organization. The whole concept of knowledge management is to capture one of the most valuable assets within any organization: the knowledge, expertise and past experiences of its employees.

In this chapter you will be provided with the basic building blocks for implementing a knowledge management solution within your organization. If implemented correctly, your organization can realize increased employee productivity as well as the collaboration and sharing of knowledge, which can translate into increased customer satisfaction with your services. The key is how your company will approach a knowledge management project from the start—technology is only one small aspect of the project. Before your organization starts evaluating technology, you must obtain senior management's buy-in and recognize that your largest challenge will be the cultural changes necessary for your project to succeed.

Defining Knowledge Management

Before we define Knowledge Management, it is important to understand a few other definitions:
- Data
    Raw facts
- Information
    A collection of related data with context and perspective
- Knowledge
    Organized information that provides guidance or action
- Wisdom
    The understanding that permits knowledge to be used

There are two types of knowledge: explicit and tacit. Explicit knowledge can be captured and shared. It can be written and when read, understood by the reader. Tacit knowledge resides within a person. It guides our behaviors and is a result of people being able to relate various experiences. Our reference to knowledge in this chapter will refer to explicit knowledge.

When a support analyst has access to knowledge, they quickly can assist customers with problems and inquiries. If analysts were limited to only data or information, then they would have to go through a trial-and-error process to resolve the problem. Once analysts have identified a solution, they will have created knowledge by determining what information was used to resolve the problem.

Knowledge management is a methodology for capturing, optimizing, delivering and maintaining a collection of knowledge that is of value to an organization. This collection is referred to as a knowledge base. Value is realized when the knowledge base is combined with the means of accessing that information in order to answer questions and solve problems in a timely fashion.

The most basic form of a knowledge base is a list of frequently asked questions (FAQs). A simple FAQ list need not utilize a database or search engine. More complex knowledge management applications will store the information in a database and refer to this database as a knowledge base. Access to the knowledge will be through a search engine. We will discuss various types of search technologies later in the chapter.

Support analysts access the knowledge base to respond to customer inquiries. By utilizing the knowledge base, they can minimize the research time to answer a question and leverage the fact that another person in the organization has already developed the answer. This is generally the first step a Level 1 support analyst takes in the resolution process. If the solution is not in the knowledge base, then the analyst would continue on with the resolution process.

A growing trend in the industry is to provide customers with direct access to the knowledge base to find answers to their own questions. This is a form of self-service that is also referred to as tier zero or Level 0 support.

Knowledge Management for the Support Center

The goal of every support center and customer support organization is to provide accurate and timely answers to their customer's questions. Each customer interaction with the support center is a "moment of truth" and as a result, the support center is being judged during every service transaction.

Support centers are continually under demand to handle an ever-increasing case volume of more complex problems without an increase in head count. This situation also makes it increasingly difficult to get advanced training even if the budget exists to do so. Technology improvement projects are also being closely scrutinized to ensure tangible bottom line impact to improved customer service without increasing headcount or recurring costs.

So, What can Knowledge Management do for the Support Center?

- Helps address the gap between rising demands and the reality of decreasing support budgets.
- Reduces analyst average talk time and thus increase the case handling capability of the team as a whole. The time to research a problem is minimized when the answer is already known to the organization. This permits support analysts to handle more cases and/or work on more difficult cases.
- Improves the accuracy and speed with which the support center can determine the root of the problem and apply a solution.
- Customers get the same quality answer to their question independent of the support analyst they communicate with.
- Increases customer satisfaction levels of the support center customers.
- Problems are resolved by Level 1 support analysts, minimizing the need to elevate cases to the more experienced and costly support organizations.
- When problems are solved on the first contact, the cost and time related to callbacks is virtually eliminated.
- Support analysts can respond to a broader range of questions without the need for expensive on-going training.
- Support analysts job satisfaction improves as they spend more time working on the more challenging cases. This results in a reduction of job burnout, thus increasing employee morale and retention.
- New support analysts can quickly become productive in a support center, minimizing the initial training requirements and costs. New analysts can relatively quickly, resolve cases based on the experiences captured by other analysts.

- The knowledge base serves as a timely tool for training for support analysts learning new products.
- Knowledge is captured as the company's intellectual asset. That knowledge can be leveraged to answer questions long after the person with the original knowledge set has moved on.
- Problems can be researched and solved once, minimizing the cost of support for those problems. Without a knowledge base, multiple support analysts commonly solve the same problem, and many times, with varied results.

Keys to Implementing an Effective Knowledge Management Solution

- The first priority is to have senior management support of the KM initiative as well as buy in from all levels of management and all staff members that will be involved in this initiative.
- Develop processes and procedures on how the knowledge base will be created and maintained.
- Ensure the tools being utilized integrate well with other systems being used. For example, if the knowledge base is not tightly integrated with the problem management system, this could make it cumbersome for the support analysts resulting in little motivation to use it consistently.
- As with any successful project, training is critical. Attention needs paid to ensuring adequate high quality training is provided to everyone who will develop, utilize and maintain the knowledge base throughout the company.

Knowledge Management for the Customers

This is commonly referred to as e-service and e-support. E-support solutions use Internet- or intranet-based services that can be accessed with a Web browser by a customer at any time from any place. E-support solutions are not just limited to the FAQ pages of the past, but have grown to include access to a company's knowledge base, checking status of an open case or request, requesting new services, engaging in a live chat with a support analyst and more.

The concept of using Web technology to allow people to help themselves is quickly becoming a service differentiator in our highly competitive global economy. The primary reason most organizations develop a support Web site for their customers is to allow customers quick, efficient and direct access to the resources they need.

Giving customers direct access to an easy-to-use, robust and accurate intranet—or Internet—based knowledge management solution has significant benefits:

- Customers are able to resolve problems on their own without having to contact the support center. This is known as level-zero support and is the critical component of any e-service offering.
- Improved customer satisfaction levels. As customers find that they can get the answers they need without having to open a case or send an e-mail to the support center, their satisfaction with the support services provided will be increased.
- Increased support-hour coverage. Customers are able to get the answers to some of their questions when they need them, 24/7…not just during the staffed hours of the support center. This may help minimize the need to add staff on off-hour shifts.
- Reduced internal costs for providing support. As more and more support questions are answered through these self-help solutions, the incoming case volume to the support center could decrease (or at least be maintained), potentially reducing the need to add future staff.

Keys to Implementing an Effective E-Support Strategy:
- Data must be kept current. Since one of the goals of e-support is to reduce the cases coming to the support organization, the e-support knowledge base must be kept up to date. In many industries, new products or services are being offered continually. Therefore, it is critical that customers can go to the e-support site and get answers and solutions for the new products and services they receive from your organization. If customers find that your knowledge base is not being kept current, they will stop using it.
- The site must be easy for customers to use. It must be intuitive, have a simple interface and be developed with commonly accepted navigation tools. A key to ease of use is to have strong search capabilities that not only include standard keyword matching, but also offer natural language searching capabilities.

The displayed results must be able to fit on a standard screen width. Customers need to be able to refine their search if the answer they are looking for is not found with the first search results.

- Give customers options. If customers cannot find the answers to the questions they are looking for, they must be able to submit questions to your support organization from the site.
- The site must be easy to administer. Ideally this e-support site is tied to the main corporate support knowledge base and is being administered by a central team. As stated above, the key is keeping the data current and if the process of administration is complex and time-consuming, you can be sure the data will not be up to date.

Proactive vs. Reactive Knowledge Management Methodologies

As with any new practice, you can choose to be either reactive or proactive. Both reactive and proactive knowledge management methodologies add value and need to be utilized in your knowledge management practice. By understanding how each methodology adds value, you can successfully implement the practices in your support center.

Reactive knowledge management is also referred to as solution-centered support or knowledge-centered support. The Consortium for Service Innovation (www.serviceinnovation.org) first introduced these terms in an attempt to educate support managers on the value of capturing and utilizing knowledge in the contact center.

Reactive knowledge management promotes capturing a solution at the time it is created and making that solution available to the support center so it won't have to be recreated. We call this reactive because a solution is created in response to a problem already occurring and being reported to the support center.

Let's walk through the process in a little more detail. A customer contacts the support center asking how to insert a table in a Word document. The support analyst is unfamiliar with this feature and does not find an existing solution in the knowledge base. After researching the question, the analyst finds the answer, informs the customer and closes the case. Normally the analyst would then be available to take another call. Unfortunately the work—researching and developing a solution— would have been used once and then discarded. In reactive knowledge management, the analyst realizes that they have created a new solution— a company asset—and documents the new knowledge. Once the question and solution is documented, it becomes available for other analysts to reuse.

The key benefit for reactive knowledge management is the lower cost of ownership. Knowledge is created as part of the support process and immediately is made available to other analysts. The disadvantages of this method relate to quality. Support analysts are rarely hired for their writing skills; you can expect to find grammar and spelling errors in the knowledge. What if the solution they provided did not actually fix the problem? Your knowledge base now contains solutions that are wrong. It is not uncommon in reactive knowledge management practices to have redundancy and multiple answers to the same question. If the solution was in the knowledge base and the analyst did not find it, then they are adding the same or a different solution to the same problem. All of these problems can be overcome by introducing a quality review process for the new knowledge. We will review this process later in the chapter.

The result of pure reactive knowledge management is a knowledge base of solutions to known problems. The solutions with the highest reuse are your frequently asked questions. The knowledge base will cover a wide variety of topics with very little depth in any given area. Sometimes depth of knowledge is desirable, such as for a new product launch where the questions could vary widely. This is where proactive knowledge management can provide value.

We refer to the methodology of building knowledge prior to its need as "proactive knowledge management". The goal is to forecast the potential questions and problems before they occur and build the knowledge base of answers and solutions in advance. The methodology follows a process similar to that of software development and includes three major phases: design, develop and deliver.

In the design phase, you develop the requirements for the knowledge base and determine how the knowledge will be organized. It is during this phase that you forecast what questions or problems will need to be answered. Researching the type of problems encountered with similar products or previous version can provide a wealth of questions.

Once you start authoring answers to these questions, you are in the development phase. During this phase you will test the accuracy of the solutions, which is referred to as validation. By enlisting a knowledge engineer in the process, you can ensure that the standards and writing formats can be achieved. The delivery of the knowledge base can then be coordinated with the release of a new product or service.

Imagine that your support center is about to rollout a new release of Microsoft Windows along with a proprietary application. To minimize the impact on the support center, the company has decided to release a knowledge base for both products on the company's intranet site. Proactive knowledge management will be used to develop the knowledge base. The knowledge engineers will work closely with the software developers, quality assurance analysts and documentation team to design and develop the knowledge base. After the project is implemented and the support center starts receiving cases, the reactive knowledge management process will be introduced to add new knowledge to the existing knowledge base. The new knowledge added should be directed to the knowledge engineers to validate the solutions and ensure consistent assembly of knowledge, prior to the introduction for production access.

Combining reactive and proactive knowledge management processes will allow your support center to achieve and maintain a quality knowledge base.

Creating Quality Knowledge
The next six steps provide you with some information for producing a quality knowledge base:

Define the problem space
You should start by identifying all of the potential problems that may result in a case to the support center. Why spend the effort adding knowl-

edge that no one will ever read? For example, establish a goal to include all the cases that generate 80 percent of the case volume. You will most likely find that 20 percent of the problems generate 80 percent of the volume.

Define the scope of your knowledge base

When you market a knowledge base, you need to make sure that you have coverage for what you market. You cannot claim to have a knowledge base for Microsoft Windows 2000 when you only have 20 FAQs. However, you can claim to have the most common FAQs for Windows 2000.

Review the articles for usability and understanding—edit for your audience

You should always remember who your audience is. This will help you determine the level of detail to include and the language that you can use. You should not tell a customer to "reinstall Windows" without providing the steps to accomplish this task. You may need to add screen shots or hypertext to provide more detail or to accommodate a less knowledgeable audience. Remember to keep screen shots small because of Internet performance.

Organize and tag content for quick access

When organizing your content, try to think like a customer. Then link the solution to the appropriate places in the knowledge base. You also have to consider what search tools will be used to retrieve the answers. Tagging a solution with classification information like Hardware, Software and Printing, helps customers find it quickly. Adding multiple symptoms and appropriate keywords improves the likelihood of finding an answer. Remember that customers look for information in many ways and in different contexts. When you provide an answer to an error message, include the exact error message in the content. This not only helps in searching for an answer, but also confirms to the customer that you have identified the correct problem.

Engineer diagnostics or troubleshooters

Sometimes customers are not able to describe a problem with

sufficient detail for you to be able to provide an answer. In these cases, you need to ask additional questions to determine what the real problem is. Once you understand the problem, you can provide the answer. Ask questions that can be confirmed by the customer, providing the steps necessary to answer the question. For example, if you ask the customer how much disk space is left, include an explanation of how he/she would obtain this information.

Establish and Follow Knowledge Management (KM) Format and Writing Standards

You will need to establish and adhere to KM format and writing standards. This is a must for any company that wants to achieve high quality in its knowledge bases. You do not need to develop standards from scratch; there are many sources for writing standards. If you are writing about proprietary products, you might check with your marketing department for standards used in product literature or with your documentation department for standards used in producing manuals. Most support centers are supporting products from a company like Microsoft. Software manufacturers may also publish the standards guides they utilize internally.

Determine What Type of Knowledge Management Best Suits Your Needs

What solutions should be added to the knowledge base? In reactive knowledge management, we said that a solution is added in response to a question. Determining what solutions to include in a knowledge base becomes more complicated when you are trying to proactively add knowledge.

Consider if you were to plot all of your answers on a grid, with the X axis representing the Frequency of Reuse and the Y axis being the Complexity of Problems. We look at Frequency of Reuse to indicate potential value. Answers with a high reuse have a high return on invest. By looking at the Complexity of Problems, we are taking into consideration the potential cost for creating the solution. Complex problems are harder to solve, requiring more diagnostics and more detailed information. To determine the potential frequency of reuse, you might research actual reuse counts for problems from a similar product.

107

Table 1

Using Table 1, all of the solutions that fall into the lower left-hand quadrant would be considered simple to solve and have a lower reuse factor. If you were to reward support analysts for the number of solutions that they add to a knowledge base, you would end up with a high number of these. Because the simple solutions are easy to author, the support analyst is able to produce more of them and get a higher reward. Unfortunately, these answers have a low reuse and the return on investment is also low. This is the quadrant that you should not focus on during proactive knowledge management, but rather allow reactive knowledge management to fill this need.

The lower right-hand quadrant contains the answers to the frequently asked questions that an experienced support analyst is easily able to answer. Because these solutions are easy to author and will be used frequently, this is a must-have quadrant. New support analysts and customers performing self-service will utilize this knowledge.

The upper right-hand quadrant contains the complex problems that are asked frequently. The cost for supporting these problems is generally high, so by capturing this knowledge you can quickly reduce the cost of support. These are the problems generally resolved by the Level 2 or Level 3 support professional. Making this knowledge available directly to customers or to the Level 1 support analysts minimizes the escalations to the Level 2 or Level 3 personnel, who are typically more costly resources. Investing in adding these answers to your knowledge base will improve the return on investment for knowledge management.

When it comes to the upper left-hand quadrant, more questions need to be asked to determine if these solutions should be captured. Remember that the cost of authoring this knowledge is high and if the solutions are not used, then you have spent company resources with little to no return. If the product being supported has a short life cycle, you may elect not to invest in this quadrant. On the other hand, if the product will be on the market for many years, then the investment cost can be easily justified; years later when the problem recurs, the people experienced with the product may no longer be available. Therefore, the costs for developing a solution in the future would be higher than developing it today. Another consideration may be the potential cost of not having an answer available. If the problem is not resolved quickly, there could be costs to the company. Investing in creating the solution today would reduce these types of risks. There is no easy rule for complex problems with low reuse. You need to look closely at your business to determine the right investment level.

When you are looking at what knowledge is key to your organization, you might ask yourself a few questions:
- What does the company lose when a person leaves the company or his/her current position?
- What is it that you have to teach every new person?
- What questions does the support center consistently receive?
- What knowledge can you not do without?

Tips and Techniques for Developing Quality Knowledge
Tips for adding screen shots
Screen shots can add clarity to a process. A support analyst or customer gains comfort when they can visually see a picture that looks similar to what they are seeing on their monitor. A screen shot can allow a support analyst to describe to customers what their monitor should look like, even

if the support analyst does not have access to the application the customer is using.

- Keep the images (JPEGs) small. Large screen shots require longer download time over the Internet.
- Add screen shots only when they are really necessary. Adding too many graphics will only slow the resolution process for customers with limited bandwidth.
- Use Windows default colors. For consistency's sake, do not change the colors from screen shot to screen shot. Varying the color schemes can cause customers to lose focus on the information itself. Using the Windows default color scheme provides a sense of familiarity. (This policy also prevents the creative minds from generating some new form of art.)
- Define a standard for annotations. Always use the same font, color and background color when adding text.
- Highlight with ovals any areas of focus on the screenshot. Use of ovals draws attention to and makes the area of focus stand out. Use the same line color and weight whenever you add this type of focus.
- Crop the screen shots. Adding a small black border around a screen shot can improve its appearance.
- Microsoft Paint works well for annotating and cropping screen shots. Tips for providing instructional steps are used to guide the support analyst or customer through a process. By segmenting the instructions into steps, it is easy to perform the process while reading the information.

Tips for providing instructional steps

- Always use the same numbering scheme, such as 1. 2. 3. ...If outlining varies from answer to answer, your knowledge base will look like multiple authors wrote it.
- Indent outline substeps consistently. Indenting substeps makes it easier for the reader to follow the procedure.
- Never have a one-step process. When a procedure involves only one step, numbering is inappropriate.

Tips for adding notes

Notes are used to emphasize information that the support analyst or customer needs to be aware of before continuing with the implementation of a solution, or to share information with them that is not directly part of the solution.

- When you include more than one note, number them for easy reference. Use a consistent numbering scheme such as Note 1, Note 2, Note 3.
- Place a note near the information that warrants it. If all notes are at the end, they probably will not be read at the time they are needed. Placing them at the end also makes it difficult to tell where they apply.
- Special notes such as WARNING or CAUTION should carry a consistent meaning. "Caution" implies that you may damage your computer or data; "Warning" implies that you may damage you. Remember: "Caution" is for computer, "Warning" is for workers.
- Another type of comment note is EXAMPLE.
- You may want to highlight notes in a different color or font to make them stand out. If you decide to do this, be consistent.

Tips for controlling the length of a solution

Controlling the length of a solution can minimize the amount of information that the support analyst or customer must review. This can also improve system performance when accessing the knowledge base.

- Provide the information necessary to solve the problem; limit the offering of alternative suggestions. Support analysts or customers are generally looking for quick answers, not for training on the multiple ways to perform a task.
- Examples are helpful, but using too many will lengthen your solution unnecessarily. Be careful not to provide more examples than answers.
- Place long examples in hypertext. Support analysts or customers can read them if they choose to.
- Place common procedures in hypertext. If the procedure is one that is commonly used in other answers, you can write it just once, as a hypertext file that can be linked to other solutions.

Tips for developing troubleshooters or diagnostics

Troubleshooters are used to walk the support analyst or customer through a discovery process, which will vary depending on the additional information the customer provides. This is generally done to resolve a problem where the customer has identified a symptom and not a specific problem.

- Ask questions that will eliminate several possible problems all at once. For example, "Is this a network printer or a local printer?"
- Ask questions that lead to early identification of common problems. Don't assume that the support analyst or customer checked common issues first.
- Consider the cost of the question. It is cheaper to check to see that the printer is plugged in than to replace the power supply. Some questions may require a lengthy diagnostic or troubleshooting process; you would not want to start with "Reinstall Windows. Does it work now?"
- Help the support analysts or customers answer the question. If you are asking how much space is left on the hard drive, provide the steps the support analysts or customers need to determine the answer.
- Never end a diagnostic with "I don't know". Instead, recommend that the support analysts or customers escalate this problem to a support professional for assistance. If you can include a contact phone number or an e-mail option at this point, do so.

Other tips for building quality
- Agree on a writing style.
- Adhere to a format and standards guide.
- Define the components that are to be part of solutions. Some commonly used components are:
  - Title
  - Problem Description
  - Symptoms
  - Product Tags (For which products is this solution relevant?)
  - Error Message (Provide the complete text.)
  - Cause
  - Solution Summary (This will commonly be used by experts.)
  - Solution Detail (This is where any steps belong.)
  - Workaround (Use this when there is no true solution but

there is a helpful alternative.)
- Keywords (Keywords enhance searching and yield better results.)
- Assign a unique ID to each answer and never change it. This will allow repeated access and easy referencing.
- Provide a way for support analysts and customers to give you feedback so you can continually improve quality.

Knowledge Management Job Functions

When establishing a knowledge management environment, there are several positions you should consider adding to your organization. In this section we will list these positions and their basic job functions.

Knowledge Engineer Responsibilities

- Identify, capture, review, edit and insert knowledge into the support knowledge base.
- Ensure knowledge entries in the support knowledge base are up-to-date and consistent in structure and presentation:
  - Help maintain submission process; review and approve new or modified knowledge.
  - Maintain knowledge structure and organization in the system.
  - Periodically review support knowledge base identifying missing or obsolete information.
  - Work with vendors to obtain and input all applicable manuals or knowledge packs.
- Use discretion and judgment to promptly organize and perform requested assignments.
- Use effective written and oral communication skills to:
  - Prepare and submit comprehensive status reports on current activities and assignments.
  - Document, review, edit and publish knowledge base entries.
  - Keep departmental contacts and supervisors informed of status on submitted knowledge base entries.
  - Set appropriate expectations with departmental contacts.

- Establish and maintain working relationships with all departments within IT to capture and share knowledge.
- Maintain knowledge of current knowledge management practices, relevant product offerings, support policies and procedures.

Knowledge Manager Responsibilities

- Ensure knowledge entries in the support knowledge base are up to date and consistent in structure and presentation:
  - Maintain submission process; review and approve new or modified knowledge.
  - Maintain knowledge structure and organization in the system.
  - Periodically review support knowledge base, identifying missing or obsolete information, and facilitate that review by others.
- Work with vendors to obtain and input all applicable manuals or packaged knowledge content.
- Use effective written and oral communication skills to:
  - Prepare and submit comprehensive status reports on current activities and assignments.
  - Prepare and submit employee performance evaluations and annual reviews.
  - Keep departmental contacts and supervisors informed of status on submitted knowledge base entries and knowledge management initiatives.
  - Set appropriate expectations with management and departmental contacts.
  - Respond to questions from managers, end-users and peers.
- Ensure all users are trained in the use of the support knowledge bases.
- Establish and maintain working relationships with all departments within IT.
- Use discretion and judgment to promptly organize and perform requested assignments.
- Monitor the knowledge management team's work queue to

ensure timely completion of knowledge base submissions.
- Plan, assign, coordinate, monitor and direct work.
  - Schedule staff hours and assignments.
  - Approve vacation and personal days; enforce company policies, including accurate record keeping of sick, personal and vacation time taken.
  - Monitor and check teamwork queues to ensure timely completion of work.
  - Ensure that Information Systems standards are always maintained.
- Develop, mentor, coach and train subordinates, ensuring environment is conducive to professional growth and technical development.
- Interview, hire and coach employees; reward and discipline staff; prepare performance evaluations and recommend salary increases.
- Obtain and prepare essential equipment and supplies for new employees; this includes computer equipment, desk supplies and necessary access to enterprise information systems.
- Maintain knowledge of current knowledge management practices, relevant product offerings, and support policies and procedures.

Workflow Process

To create quality knowledge, a number of people may be involved. In this section, we will provide examples of workflow processes used for both reactive and proactive knowledge management. The reason for using a workflow process is to manage the passing of work from one person to another. Multiple people are involved to ensure that the person with the right competency is performing the appropriate task.

Reactive Knowledge Management Workflow

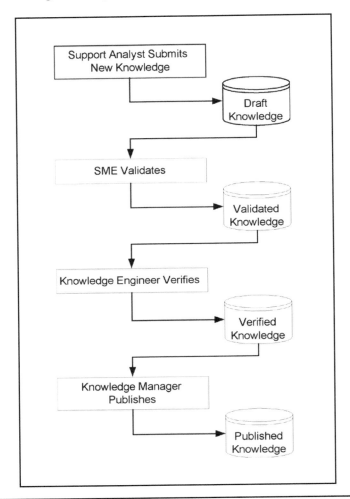

Figure 1

You may recall that in a reactive KM process the knowledge is captured in response to a problem being reported to the support center.

The support analyst who resolves the problem has just created a new solution. He/She creates the first draft of the knowledge by recording information about the problem and the solutions, including as much pertinent information as possible, like the version of the software and the symptoms resulting from the problem. It is not important to include who reported the problem or any information about the customer; only information related to the actual problem.

A subject-matter expert (SME) should then validate the problem and solution. The SME is most likely a Level 2 or Level 3 support analyst with specific knowledge of the domain to which the knowledge belongs. It is the SME's responsibility to make sure the solution is correct and that all of the necessary information was collected. SMEs may also classify or categorize the knowledge in the knowledge base for quick access and easier management. It is also their task to eliminate redundancy. A knowledge engineer will then verify the knowledge for grammar, spelling, writing style and presentation format so that the agreed to standards are followed. While the SME ensured content accuracy, the knowledge engineer makes sure the information is comprehensible. The knowledge engineer may also add information such as definition, hypertext, screen shots or examples to help clarify the knowledge.

The knowledge is now ready to be published. The knowledge manager or knowledge engineer defines the rules for when new knowledge can be shared with customers. Depending on the technology used, they may need to actually publish a copy of the knowledge and move it to the Internet site.

In a reactive knowledge management process, the task of capturing new knowledge becomes part of the case-management practice—that is, new knowledge is captured when a case is closed. The review of the knowledge by a subject-matter expert and a knowledge engineer increases the quality of the knowledge.

Proactive Knowledge Management Workflow

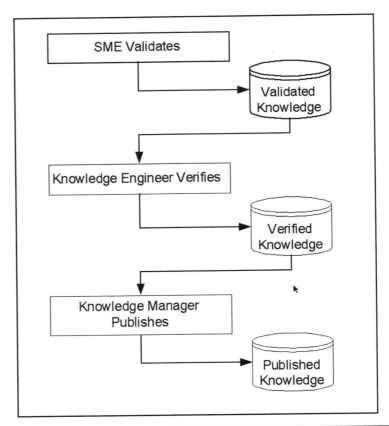

Figure 2

The process followed for proactive knowledge management is only slightly different. The same key steps of capturing, validating, verifying and publishing exist within this process. In proactive knowledge management, we discussed the steps of design, develop and deliver. This workflow process focuses on the develop step.

An SME submits the new knowledge. This may be a software developer as they create the software or someone testing the software. It could be assumed that the SME is both capturing and validating the knowledge. The SME will also classify the information in the knowledge base for easy access and management.

The knowledge engineer will then test the new knowledge, if possible, and rewrite the knowledge according to the agreed-upon standards. If the knowledge engineer is capable of reproducing the problem, then he/she will use the solution provided to resolve the problem. In this way the knowledge engineer will have validated the knowledge and come to understand it. By adding the additional information to help a reader understand the knowledge, the knowledge engineer verifies the knowledge.

The knowledge is now ready to be published. The knowledge manager or knowledge engineer defines the rules for when new knowledge can be shared with customers. Depending on the technology used, they may need to actually publish a copy of the knowledge and/or move it to the Internet site.

Some companies may elect to add an additional task in both of the above processes. This task is commonly referred to as an edit. A copy editor will be the final person to read and possibly test the solution. Just as the knowledge engineer checks the subject-matter expert's work, the copy editor checks that the knowledge engineer properly did his/her work. Quality is the primary reason for adding this additional cost to the process of creating knowledge.

Steps to Successfully Implement Knowledge Management

The first step many managers take when asked to implement knowledge management is to investigate the vendors. Approaching a project such as knowledge management should never begin with the technology. Below is a brief overview of some of the key steps necessary to successfully implement knowledge management within your support center.

Define the business objectives. Understanding why you have been asked to implement knowledge management is the first step in the project. What are the expectations of management for the project? Is the goal to reduce your budget? If so, you might need to educate your management. The project can save money by reducing the cost of support on a per-case basis, but you have to remember that the support demands are going up.

Implementing knowledge management is a step for managing the rising support costs, not a step that will reduce costs. Perhaps the goals are customer satisfaction or customer retention. Whatever the goals are, you need to understand them, develop a plan to measure them and ensure you deliver on the defined business objectives.

Once you know why you are implementing knowledge management, you need to secure a management champion. Generally this is the sponsor of the project. A champion is someone with enough authority and resources to support the project. This individual understands the ultimate business gains and can communicate the vision. The champion will also support you when things are not going exactly as planned.

The third step is to understand your customer. Do you know who your audience is? Who will have access to the knowledge base? Supporting field technicians and supporting customers require different things. Do you need to provide global support or 24/7 support? Understanding who the customers are will help define the requirements for both the content in the knowledge base as well as the functionality of the technology. At this point you can propose what your new service levels may be, once self-service knowledge management is implemented.

You should model the workflows that you will be implementing. Make sure to consider the various contact points to the support center. Here is a simple example; however, you will need to be more detailed in your plan.

Customers have a choice to check the Web, call the support center or send an e-mail. If they check the Web, then they are presented with the ability to search or browse the knowledge base. If they find a solution,then the workflow is complete. If they do not find a solution, then they are presented with an option to escalate the problem to the support center. The escalation could be done via an e-mail to the support center, with an automatic e-mail confirmation to the customer that the support center will respond to all e-mails with-in 1 hour between the hours of 7:00 a.m. and 9:00 p.m. Monday through Friday. If this is an emergency, the customer is requested to call the support center at 800-321-HELP for after-hours support.

You need to consider the impact of implementing knowledge management on your various audiences. Do not simply focus on how they will use these new tools, but on how it will alter the way you are providing support.

Now it is time to visit with vendors and evaluate the technology options. Share with them your vision and allow them to demonstrate to you how their tool can support and possibly enhance that vision. You most likely have already invested in technology within your support center. Ask to see working examples of the vendor's products working with your existingtools, such as your problem-management system. You should also talk with the vendor's existing customers to hear about their implementation and use of these tools; you may learn about other options that will allow you to enhance your plans.When selecting a vendor, remember that you are looking for a service partner—someone that will help you ensure success.

Implementing in phases will reduce your risk. You need to have a problem-management system in place to manage and track the problems, questions and inquiries your customers contact you about. You need a knowledge management system to capture and deliver the answers your support center is creating. That does not mean you have to provide a knowledge base for every product you support. You might elect to implement knowledge management within the support center first and provide customer access in a later phase. This allows you to get it right internally before you make it visible to customers. Your first knowledge base may be related to a new product you are supporting. By limiting the scope of the knowledge base, you may be reducing the number of people involved in the initial project. This also allows you to work through the processes with a small team before rolling out the changes to a larger audience.

Something to evaluate when implementing self-service are the additional functionalities you are considering within your project plan. You may elect to implement e-mail escalation first and then later follow that with chat. This allows you to work out the e-mail support process and measurements before you add another service to your offering.

Implementing knowledge management is a cultural change for the support center. You will need to utilize your change management skills to help people understand and support the project. Some will fear the loss of their jobs instead of recognizing how their roles are being expanded. Because the skills required are changing, you may need to provide some specialized training beyond the tools and process. For example, good writing skills are essential for personnel responding to e-mail or chat. Capturing and validating knowledge may also be new to your staff.

Marketing is a key component to your change management initiative. You need to educate your staff and your customers on the value of your enhanced service so that they use it and provide you with feedback.

When you implement knowledge management, you need to re-evaluate the performance metrics that exist within your organization. If people are rewarded for the number of cases they handle, they are going to resist process changes that will lengthen the time to close a case, such as capturing the knowledge. We will cover managing change in more detail later in the chapter.

You should define the measurements that allow you to manage the process and determine if you are meeting objectives. You will need to add new measurements and adjust existing measures to ensure a balance. While most support centers are proud of their first-case resolution rates, implementing knowledge management tends to lower that rate because the customer is resolving the simple cases using self-service and the support analyst is resolving more challenging questions.

You will need to measure, make adjustment and then measure again. Once you are satisfied with the progress, you will be able to move on to the next phase of the project.

Managing Change

The number-one reason most knowledge management implementations fail has nothing to do with the technology. Most failures occur because the resistance to change was not managed. The staff that had to make the changes to the processes were not in full support of the project.

There have been many books written on change management and we are not going to try to cover this topic in detail within this book. We will share with you some things to consider when preparing to manage change during a knowledge management implementation.

- The support professionals fear they will lose their job. Management is going to use this new technology to reduce staff. You need to explain the true objectives and how people are critical to making the project successful.
- The support analyst likes things as they are. You can't satisfy this one, because things have to change. As part of the implementation you should update the job descriptions to support the new processes and objectives.
- The support analysts do not want to share their knowledge out of fear that it will detract from their value as employees. It is true that their knowledge adds value, but they can add more value to the company by sharing that knowledge. You might want to consider rewards and special recognition for people who make valuable contributions to the knowledge base.
- Support analysts are expected to answer 30 cases per day and this is going to be more work. You have to change the focus of the organization. The number of cases per support analyst may go down for a while. You need to review your performance measurements to make sure you are not encouraging resistance, but rather are promoting change.
- People want to see career growth. By expanding their roles and creating new roles within the support organization, such as knowledge engineer, you are increasing their value and opportunities.
- People want to learn and do a good job. This is especially true with support analysts. For them to do a good job, you will need to define what that means. Developing quality standards for knowledge will clarify to your staff what the requirements are. You will need to provide them with training on the new tools and processes. You may also need to provide them skills training, such as writing and knowledge capturing.

- People want to be involved. This is a project that can provide a variety of opportunity for people to be involved and provide leadership opportunities. If you make this their project, they will help you be successful.

Did you hire the right staff? Most support center managers do not hire people for their writing skills or knowledge engineering skills. That does not mean you have the wrong staff, but you may not have the competencies necessary to be successful. It may be necessary to augment your staff or to provide additional training. Take a close look at what skills you will need to implement and manage a knowledge management initiative, and make sure you have the right competencies within your team.

If you have been given the responsibility and the authority to implement knowledge management, then make sure you have the resources and the ability to succeed. Utilize change-management practices to minimize resistance to the project and to build support where needed.

Measurements

If you do not measure it, you cannot adequately manage it. Support center managers learned this lesson a long time ago. They have come to depend on measurements from their ACD systems, problem-management systems, and e-mail management systems to ensure they are meeting their service level agreements (SLAs) and to enable them to better manage people and processes. The same needs exist when you implement knowledge management. Not only do you need new measurements, you need to review the impact of knowledge management to you existing measurements. Unfortunately most of the knowledge management vendors have not understood the value support center managers place on measurements and reporting. You will need to look closely at the reports provided by the vendor and be prepared to have to develop some on your own. The measurement itself may have little value until you trend a number of measurements over time to determine relationship and improvements.

Many companies have implemented survey buttons on the Web when a customer reads a solution. However, customer usage of the survey buttons has been low, requiring support centers to evaluate other measurements. When analyzing the value of the knowledge base, you may look at measures like:

- Total number of solutions available
- Number of cases resolved using the knowledge base
- Percent of cases resolved using the knowledge base
- Number of times customers access the knowledge base
- Number of escalations to the support center via the Web; you can then monitor the percent of escalation per customer visits
- Frequently accessed questions in the knowledge base provide great feedback to development and other departments
- Number of solutions contributed by various teams or departments compared to the resolution rates for those subjects via the knowledge base

You may want to review some of your existing measurements.

- Case volume per contact channel. How are customers contacting the support center? Hopefully you will see an increase in Web access. Your percent of phone cases should go down.
- First-case resolution rate. When you implement knowledge management for support analysts, the first-case resolution rate should increase as analysts answer more cases more quickly. When you implement customer self-service, the first-case resolution rate should decrease as customers start answering their own questions, leaving the more challenging cases for the support center. You will need to be able to integrate your self-service measures into your measurement and reporting process.
- Average case duration. When you first implement knowledge management, there is a learning curve and the time to handle a case will increase. As the support analysts become more comfortable with the tools and the knowledge base contains more information, this time will begin to decrease again. Keep in mind that you are also asking support analysts to do more work (capture the knowledge) when a solution is not in the knowledge base. This will extend the time spent on this case, but the time will be leveraged the next time a customer presents the same

problem. After you implement self-service and customers are solving more problems on their own, the support center is left with the more challenging cases that may take longer to solve.

Reporting

Since you are implementing new processes such as the workflow process for enhancing the quality of a newly contributed piece of knowledge, you will need reports to manage those processes.

- The number of solutions at each stage in the workflow. This is the work in progress and shows the backlog of work to be done.
- The average age of a solution at each stage in the workflow. This allows you to see how long it takes to do the work, as well as identifies bottlenecks in the process.
- The number of solutions rejected at various stages in the workflow. This allows you to identify rework costs and potential problems with the knowledge-capturing task.
- You may want to be able to see these types of measurements by knowledge engineer, by a team of people or perhaps by knowledge domains. The cost of writing knowledge for one domain may be very different from another domain, such as network support vs. Microsoft Office support.

Implementing measurements early in the process will allow you to identify issues so that you can make adjustments. In addition to these types of measurements, make sure you are capturing the measurements that will be used to define the project's success.

Technology

When you begin to evaluate the various technologies, it is important to remember the different customers of your knowledge management initiative. Let's consider four different audiences for one implementation and the types of needs they have.

Customers

- search and/or browse the knowledge base
- print, save or e-mail a piece of knowledge
- escalate problem to the support center along with history of what they attempted to do
- provide feedback on existing or new knowledge

Support Analyst

- browse and perform advanced searches on the knowledge base
- print, save or e-mail a piece of knowledge
- escalate problem along with history of the work they have done
- provide feedback on existing knowledge
- contribute new knowledge
- close a customer case with the appropriate documentation

Knowledge Engineer

- browse and perform advanced searches on the knowledge base
- print, save or e-mail a piece of knowledge
- author new knowledge
- accept or reject knowledge submitted by others
- manage (organize, edit, delete or archive) existing knowledge
- provide workflow support for managing the quality process
- publish knowledge to the support center and/or Web

Knowledge Manager

- monitor and measure usage
- monitor and measure knowledge within the workflow
- secure knowledge based on audience or business rules

You need to evaluate the technology and how it will affect the needs of the different audiences within your implementation.

Various Search Methods

Different audiences will also search the knowledge differently. Some vendors support multiple search methodologies using the same knowledge base, allowing the support analyst or customer to choose the search method that best meets his/her needs. You may be familiar with some of these methods.

Decision Tree

A decision tree is a common method of searching that can guide the support analyst or customer to a solution. A simple decision tree might be a categorized list of FAQs. On the first page, the support analyst or customer would select the product they are having trouble with. The system would then present a list of FAQs for that product. Another type of decision tree is referred to as a diagnostic tree or troubleshooter. In this case, the support analyst or customer is presented with a question that helps the system identify the actual problem. The answer may lead to a solution or to another question. Diagnostic trees are an easy way to guide the support analyst or the customer from a symptom like "I can't print" to a problem like "I can't print because my printer is out of paper". A solution can be provided for the latter.

Keyword Search

A keyword search was an early search method used by many Web sites. The support analyst or customer types a small number of words into a search string and clicks on the "Search" button. The system then returns a list of answers or pages that contain one or more of the words provided. The more words that matched the contents of the search string, the higher the relevance given the answer. Advances in keyword search engines include stemming. Stemming is an algorithm that matches a word like "Print" with "Prints," "Printing" and "Printer". Advanced keyword search engines allow for options like Boolean operators such as AND, OR and NOT.

Natural-Language Processing

Advances in keyword search engines have lead to more sophisticated search capabilities that allow the support analyst or customer to enter phrases or sentences. These systems evaluate the words based on their positioning to each other. An exact match of a phrase would have a higher relevancy than phrases with all the same words in a different order. Natural-language processors usually support features similar to keyword searches, in addition to having a thesaurus, phonetic spelling capabilities, and ignore or stop words (in addition to other advances). Natural-language processing is the easiest for most non-technical users and is enjoying wide popularity and support on the Web.

Associative Search

Answers also can be found by identifying specific facts, symptoms or attributes about the problem. For example: The support analyst or customer identifies a printing-related problem with Microsoft Word and an HP printer. The information in this example comes from a symptom, "problem printing," and the facts, "Microsoft Word" and "HP printer". The search engine would provide the support analyst or customer with a list of potential solutions where all three pieces of information have been associated with those solutions. It may also provide the ability for the support analyst or customer to add additional information that would refine the search, such as "Error message 104". More advanced forms of this type of search engine keep track of usage and then leverage those experiences to provide a relevancy weight to the solutions provided, placing the most likely solution first on the list.

Case-based Reasoning

Case-based reasoning (CBR) is similar to an associative search engine in that every solution has a number of related attributes. Solutions along with these attributes are defined as cases. A case may also include a set of diagnostic questions and answers. When the support analyst or customer types in a search string and clicks on the "Search" button, the system responds with a list of potential solutions. In addition, the system presents a set of questions that will help refine the search. The questions are usually ordered so that the first question relates to more of the solutions provided, as the system reasoned that these solutions are the most likely to resolve the problem. Unlike a decision tree, the support analyst or customer can choose to answer any question in any order. Both the selection of questions and the answers provided by the support analyst or customer impact the search results. This technology can provide for a very dynamic knowledge base. The challenge is in the authoring and management of the knowledge.

The various search technologies work against structured and unstructured knowledge bases. An unstructured knowledge base is a collection of documents in various formats, such as wrd, pdf, html, text, ppt and xls. The document contains words, but the search engine has no means for determining the context of the words. The lack of structure minimizes the ability for the search engine to provide the right answer. A search for "printing problem" will yield solutions that have nothing to do with printing. Somewhere in the document the word "print" may have been used, like "To see his name in print" or "A test print will be performed." This does not mean that unstructured knowledge is invaluable. Most companies have file servers full of documentation, brochures, manuals and other files that when combined with a search engine, permit the support analyst or customer to find a solution faster.

Structured knowledge bases are usually stored in a database or set of XML files. Each piece of knowledge contains a number of fields that provide structure. Sample fields are solution title, problem description, cause, error message, symptoms, product, solution, diagnostic questions, expiration date, create date and author. When a search for "printing problem" is done against a structured knowledge base, the search engine would analyze fields like the problem description, cause, error message, and symptom field, not the field containing the solution. Searches of structured knowledge bases tend to yield better results, allowing the support analyst or customer to find the answer quickly.

Knowledge management applications utilize structured knowledge bases to provide true management capabilities. Many vendors will also support searching unstructured knowledge as a means to leverage existing information and information that is produced by others. Some vendors provide clustering technology that can produce some level of structure from unstructured content. These technologies can categorize or cluster documents by analyzing the contents of all the documents and identifying specific words or phrases within them.

Knowledge management applications may work with online or offline knowledge bases. An online knowledge base implies that the support analysts and customers have real-time access to the knowledge. As knowledge is changed, all support analysts and customers see the change immediately. An offline knowledge base implies that there is a master copy of the knowledge base used by the knowledge engineers and that the knowledge base accessible to support analysts and customers must be published. Generally a published knowledge base is a subset of the master knowledge base, containing only the knowledge that has been through the quality process.

Let's examine another form of an online and an offline knowledge base. The simplest FAQ list is an HTML page with links to HTML pages containing commonly asked questions and answers. This static page is developed and published to the Web site. While many Web sites offer FAQs, they are manually maintained; they are updated as often as the Webmaster can get to them. Some knowledge management applications provide a publishing function that will produce the FAQ list based on usage history. This function can be scheduled so that the FAQs are updated as frequently as the administrator desires, such as weekly, daily or hourly. More advanced technology provides for dynamic FAQs that are updated as the knowledge base is used. By keeping usage records, the Web application presents the FAQs based on the usage history at the time the support analyst or customer requested to view the list of FAQs.

When you introduce knowledge management, you need to ensure that the problem-management process remains efficient and is improved. One way this is accomplished is by integrating these technologies to minimize data entry errors, enhance case documentation and improve speed. Many vendors claim to have integration capabilities with the leading problem-management systems. The definition of this varies widely by vendors: Is the integration out of the box, or does it require custom development? Does data pass between the applications? If so, what data? Look closely at how the knowledge management vendors have leveraged your existing tool set.

When evaluating knowledge management vendors, consider the following for your knowledge management initiative:
- Support for open standards. Does the vendor support MS SQL, Oracle or a proprietary database? Finding DBA support for MS SQL or Oracle is much easier.
- Integration capabilities. Will integration with your problem-management system and e-mail management system be out of the box or require custom development? What particular versions of third-party products does the vendor support? How long after a third-party product is released will a vendor provide support for the new release?
- What search methodologies does the vendor support?
- What unstructured knowledge does the vendor support?
- How easy is it to author new knowledge?
- How can support analysts and/or customers contribute to and

comment on the knowledge base?

- How scalable is it? How many concurrent support analysts and/or customers can access the knowledge base? Ask to see independently provided performance statistics.
- What are the hardware requirements?
- What management functions are available to analyze usage of the knowledge? Can knowledge have an expiration date? Can it be archived?
- What security is available for both accessing and managing the knowledge? Is security based on the knowledge base or can the knowledge be segmented according to audiences?
- Is the knowledge base accessible by customers in real time or does the knowledge base have to be published? In either case, how is this managed?
- How is redundancy managed? Can knowledge be linked or is it copied?
- What type of workflow or quality process does the application support? Is this process definable by the administrator?
- Can external knowledge be leveraged? Can you import existing knowledge? Can you link to knowledge on the Web? Can you spider a Web site?
- What personalization is available for both the knowledge engineer and the customer?
- How will the application integrate both technically and visually with your corporate Web site? Does the application support templates?
- What reporting and measurements are available out of the box? How are new reports created?
- You should also evaluate the professional services and support offerings.
- What training is available for the product and for the methodology?
- Is there a published training schedule?
- Can you purchase training materials for internal training?
- What is the vendor's SLA for support and maintenance?
- What is the warranty on custom services?
- Do they use their own product?

Whenever possible it is best to talk with other companies that have implemented the vendor's products. Ask about why they selected the vendor, the implementation, the post-implementation support, software updates, and the success and challenges of their implementation. Keep in mind that vendors will only provide references for their successful stories. You might want to find the vendor's other customers through user groups such as the Help Desk Institute.

Knowledge Management Resources and Industry Vendors

KM Publication Resources

Knowledge Management: www.kmmag.com
KM World: www.kmworld.com
Call Center Magazine: www.callcentermagazine.com
IT Support News: www.itsupportnews.com
Customer Support Magazine:
http://industryclick.com/magazine.asp?siteid=2&magazineid=52

KM Software Providers

ServiceWare: www.serviceware.com
Primus: www.primus.com
Kana (ServiceSoft acquisition): www.kana.com
EGain (Inference acquisition): www.egain.com
Knowlix: www.knowlix.com
RightNow Technologies: www.rightnowtech.com
Knowledgebase.Net: www.knowledgebase.net
Knowledge Management Software: www.kmsoftware.com
AskJeeves: www.askjeeves.com
Verity: www.verity.com
Autonomy: www.autonomy.com
Documentum: www.documentum.com
Knowledge Track Corporation: www.knowledgetrack.com
Kanisa: www.kanisa.com
Motive: www.motive.com
Support.com: www.support.com
RightAnswers: www.rightanswers.com
Attenza: www.attenza.com

Knowledge Broker, Inc: www.kbi.com
Kview: www.kview.com

KM News and Reference Resources

The KM Resource Center: www.kmresource.com
Consortium for Service Innovation: www.serviceinnovation.org
CIO Magazine: www.cio.com
News Page: www.newspage.com
Business Wire: www.businesswire.com
TechWeb: www.techweb.com
ZdNet: www.zdnet.com
KM Economics Council: www.km.org
Supportindustry.com: www.supportindustry.com
@Brint BizTech Network: www.brint.com

Chapter 12

By Malcolm Fry

Managing Global Support

In the not too distant past, global support was not a critical issue. Remote locations did not have sophisticated technology resources and were generally left to their own initiative to provide local support—sometimes with a little help from central technology departments, or in some cases large global companies had sophisticated data centers around the world that functioned independent of the corporate technology departments. In today's environment, however, global support is essential due to standard workstations, company mergers, e-commerce, office systems, global networks, Y2K issues and portable technologies (notepads). These factors and the increasing cost of support have executives evaluating global support when determining how to provide efficient and cost-effective technology.

The Challenge of Providing Global Support

The challenge of providing global support is exciting and rewarding as long as the issues and scope are fully understood. The fact that an organization has a great support desk in one country is not a guarantee that world-class global support will follow. The requirements for global support are subject to many external influences that cannot be experienced by single-country support.

Road Warriors

These intrepid warriors travel the world on corporate business, carrying their trusty notepads like gunslingers. And like gunslingers without guns, traveling executives feel exposed and vulnerable without their notepads, knowing that the opposition can kill them with one techno-bullet. One executive was flying to another country, putting the finishing touches on a presentation for the next day for a contract bid of $20 million, when his notepad failed. His reaction was to call the Help Desk from the airplane, and to his surprise and pleasure the Help Desk solved his problem within 10 minutes! He now refers to that call as the "$20-million phone call" because he is convinced that without his notepad he would have been stressed and may not have won the contract. But what if his notepad had a hardware failure? Would the Help Desk have been able to provide adequate support? Road warriors are a challenge to support because they have state-of-the-art equipment and often travel to countries where their company does not have an office. Their notepads are mission-critical tools, but road warriors are often not techno-competent and in many cases work for a company that does not provide global support. In fact, road warriors can often be difficult to support even when they travel around their own country! Supporting this traveling resource requires careful planning, global break-and-fix contracts and careful asset management.

Technology Availability

Global support would be simplified if the same levels of technology were available on a global basis, but for many reasons this is not the reality. For example, a vendor may decide not to release the latest version on a particular continent due to: marketing or availability reasons, absence of required levels of telecommunications, low spare-part stocks because the number of products is not high in a specific country, prohibitive import tariffs or undertrained engineers. These are just a few of the reasons why global technology availability is an enigma facing many global support centers. Remember, technology availability involves hardware, software and telecommunications. Solving this conundrum requires a level of planning, knowledge and co-operation far beyond the levels needed to provide local support.

Corporate Issues

Corporate issues should not be a problem but they are. One organization has had its global support strategy delayed by nearly a year due to a corporate argument between its British and German technology centers concerning the ownership of the European location of the global support center. This type of conflict can be much more difficult to resolve than some problems that at first glance seem more difficult. Without corporate unity, global support is impossible.

Culture and Language

Culture and language are among the first issues raised when the subject of global support is discussed and, although important, are given too much emphasis. In many cases the real culture and language issue relates more to corporate processes than international factors. For example, if it is required that a whole corporation speak English, then obviously the problem of language support is not as great. Culture and language are more likely to be an issue for a company providing global support to external customers (e.g., e-commerce) than a company providing global support to corporate employees. Corporate employees can be trained, be expected to speak a common language, follow corporate rules and understand the corporate culture, whereas external customers are totally unpredictable and often are just looking for an opportunity to use culture and language to create confrontation (it's amazing what people will do for a discount or refund). Therefore, the first step toward solving the language and culture problem is to clearly identify the customer base. Then issues such as language, support and cultural processes can be considered. One of the main reasons that "chasing the sun" (i.e., having global support centers on every continent) is popular is because the language and cultural issues are automatically reduced.

Cultural Motivational Factors

Motivating global support staff can provide a surprising challenge. In the ideal world, all of the global support staff would be treated exactly the same; in reality, this is not possible. For example, support center staff in the United States might be salaried and get two weeks' vacation, while European support center staffs receive four to five weeks' vacation and paternal motivation. Also, demotivation can readily occur if, for instance, the prayer requirements of some religions are not understood or are ignored. It is essential to understand both the cultural motivators and demotivators in order to build harmonious global support. Corporate issues, while not necessarily culturally based, must also be addressed as there may be some resentment directed toward the global support center's headquarters due to a perception of more opportunities for advancement, autocratic decisions and a superior attitude.

Linguistics and Translation

Multiple-language support is obviously a real concern: not only is the number of languages a problem, but also the number of agents required to support each language. Combine this with the fact that college or university fluency is not the same as colloquial fluency, and the problem becomes more challenging. Badly translated technical documents can be either amusing or downright impossible to understand. It is important to identify the difference between verbal language fluency and the ability to translate written documents; do not assume that technicians or support agents can translate technical documents.

Logistics and Locations

If multiple locations are integral to global support, then logistics and locations will need careful consideration. In fact, even a single center for global support requires careful consideration. Often the logical location for central support is at central headquarters, but this need not be the case. Another location, or indeed another country, may provide a more cost-effective and strategic solution. If multiple global support centers are to be established, where should they be located? This is usually determined by the geographical concentration of remote staff, but other factors must also be considered, such as costs, telecommunications, engineering support, local expertise, office availability and local government policies. It is obvious that the wrong choice of location can be disastrous, but the correct choice can only come from evaluating all of the options and making a sound business decision independent of corporate politics.

Finding Remote Staff/Skills

One of the most important factors to consider when choosing a location is the availability of staff and the ability to train those staff to the required levels. This is an ongoing problem and not just a start-up concern. In fact, in some ways start-up is easier because of the benefits of scale. For example, it may be cost-effective to send a skilled trainer to another country to train 10 people, but does the same criteria apply when only one new member of staff requires training? So the issue is to both find the correct quality staff and to ensure that those staff meet the required levels of skills. This can only be achieved with detailed job descriptions, clear service levels, structured training plans and standard recruitment processes. Most support centers do not have these disciplines in place at present, so some local housekeeping may be required before attempting to implement global support.

Government Concessions/Where to Locate

Many governments, especially those in Europe, sponsor new business ventures with a variety of incentives, including tax relief, salary contributions and relocation assistance. It is essential that all of these incentives are identified and evaluated before any decisions are made concerning locations. Some of the savings are considerable and usually include local government support for recruitment and training, which can also help alleviate some of the local cultural problems.

Legal, Government and Employment Issues

Legal, government and employment issues can be a minefield when establishing global support center locations abroad. Contracts are interpreted differently in many countries, so a contract appropriate in one country may not be sufficient in another. Likewise, some of the governmental restrictions can vary dramatically from country to country. For example, some European countries allow unlimited overtime hours while others place restrictions on overtime. Contracts need to be reviewed by local lawyers in countries where foreign agreements are required, but it is much better to sign a worldwide contract with one company rather than with a series of countries. This will reduce administration, eliminate a lot of negotiating and allow disputes to be resolved in the country where the contract was signed. Understanding these nuances is vital to creating global support.

Global Support Structures

Although there are many variations on a theme, there are only a few basic structural templates that can be applied to provide global support. Selecting the correct template is crucial if global support is to be a success.

Follow the Sun Support

Normally, follow the sun consists of three support centers: one on each continent (although could consist of more for very large multinational companies). The concept is that as one center closes business, the provision of support is automatically transferred to the next continent. For example: if support centers were located in the United States, the United Kingdom and Australia, when the U. S. support center finished work for the day it would transfer support to the U.K. support center, which in turn would transfer support to the Australia support center, which would then transfer support back to the U.S. support center. This cycle provides 24-hour global support. The advantage of follow the sun support is that local experts address many of the language and cultural issues. Generally only large multinational organizations with offices around the world would favor this system. Follow the sun requires that each support center be an image of the others, with the same standards, the same tool sets, the same processes, the same procedures and the same staff management disciplines. Normally one of the locations will be the parent location where overall control and management reside; this provides a focal point and a place for creating and maintaining standards while allowing the other centers to concentrate on providing support. Follow the sun does require a higher investment in logistics and premises, but technology could be centralized at one location to reduce costs and maintenance.

One Central Global Support Location

One central global support location is exactly what it says: one location supplying global support on a 24-hour basis. Providing one support center will reduce costs and overhead, but it can create issues such as language support, cultural differences and local knowledge. These issues require careful consideration and planning. Normally, local telephone numbers are provided to access centralized support so that costs are reduced to the customer, but the cost of these international calls can dramatically reduce the cost benefits. For many large multinational organizations it is a straight choice between following the sun or providing central global support— with costs, corporate culture and logistics being the deciding factors in many cases. However, companies that need to provide global support but do not have large numbers of staff working abroad are more likely to have one central global support location. Ironically, large organizations with many external customers around the world but not many staff representatives abroad also favor central global support (e.g., e-commerce). This is often because of the problems related to building resources in countries where no company expertise exists.

Country/Region Centric

This is the traditional method favored by many of the largest multi-national organizations, and it consists of each significant location having specialized local support. For example, imagine a large automobile manufacturer with 10 plants around the world: it is easy to see why such a company may favor dedicated support for each production plant. Normally country, or region, centric support centers do not pass control from one location to another, as in follow the sun, but provide all local support requirements. Although this can prove more expensive, the risk of not providing local support and, for example, stopping production lines is too great. Each centric center should use the same tool sets and embrace the same processes, procedures and staff management disciplines to reduce costs. Also, there is no reason why one of the centric centers cannot be the parent site. In some cases only the first level is country/region centric, with second-level support provided at a central location. This allows country support staff to be fully trained for local needs, while support for other problems is provided centrally (e.g., central support would manage the fixing of program problems).

Managed or Outsourcing Part/Full Support

Managed or outsourcing part/full support could be applied to all of the other structural templates. The concept in the case of partial support is to retain control at a central company-managed support center, but to outsource foreign support to local specialist organizations. This eliminates most of the cultural and language issues, but allows flexibility for growth and change while maintaining central control. In the case of full support, all support functions are outsourced to global support specialists. Managed support, often known as insourcing, means that the company employs external specialists—residing on company premises, using company staff and technologies—to manage its global support requirements. If an organization is to have its support managed or outsourced, it must first decide which template should be employed. Then careful planning and preparation is essential to manage costs and ensure that the outside party will provide the correct levels of service.

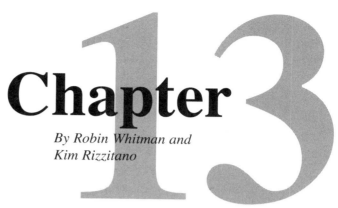

Chapter 13

*By Robin Whitman and
Kim Rizzitano*

Change Management and the Help Desk

Change management is the strategic system organizations use to manage and control the process of implementing change. In the scope of support services, changes relate to hardware, software, or communication links within a company. Change management has gained increasing importance for Help Desks, because it impacts the levels of support provided by the information services group. Help Desks should use change management strategies to minimize the negative impact to their service level agreements (SLA's) with their customers.

In this chapter, we'll discuss the importance of change management and how you can help drive this process at your Help Desk and throughout all of your company's support partners.

Change Happens

Change is constant and will happen. This is a fact. Understanding why the change is necessary is important, and understanding its affect on the organization is key. Many times, the Help Desk is the *last* to know about the changes taking place, but they are the *first* to know that there is a problem as it causes a dramatic increase in call volume.

It is important to get the Help Desk involved from the beginning.

Any project involving a change to hardware, software or communications in your organization, must have active participation by the Help Desk. This helps to create continuity in the process. Since Help Desks are the first point of contact for the customer, they have a clearer understanding of the customer's needs and their level of expertise. By working with the developers, business analysts and the others involved in a project, the Help Desk can add this incite to the project as it develops. Their expertise can also help with the formulation of training manuals, on-line documentation, web-based help and also insure that the customer and all support partners experience the least amount of impact from the change.

Hardware vs. Software

When a failure occurs within a company as a result of a change in hardware, software, or communications links, the Help Desk is often the first to know. With adequate involvement in the change management process, the Help Desk can isolate problems more readily. When something that worked yesterday is not working today, and the only difference is area of the change to the hardware or software, it becomes quickly apparent where to start the troubleshooting process.

Hardware

Maintaining a good inventory of the hardware in your organization is essential. There are many programs available, which will enable you to track hardware assets (computers, printers, etc). Some of these are tied into Help Desk call tracking software packages and others run separately. Asset management, the tracking of assets, is very important when changes are made to the way hardware and software is being used. This should be considered when working within the life cycle of a project and dealing with change management.

When dealing with a hardware change, the Help Desk can take the necessary steps to diagnose issues based on the new configuration. There are many tools available to Help Desks, which enable them to remotely control the customer's desktop computer based on an assigned asset number. Using these types of tools, the asset's configuration information can be obtained. Determining the amount of memory, hard disk size, network configuration, etc. is all extremely important when trying to diagnose error messages. By being involved in the change management process, the Help Desk agent will be aware of new hardware being rolled-out and its potential impact to the customer's computer environment.

Software

As projects develop and changes happen within software applications, these changes should be handled in the same manner as hardware changes. Many times developers have special PC's which have more memory, faster processors, etc. than the average customer. This can cause issues when a new version of software is rolled-out and locks up the customer's computer. The same is true of printing issues. If reports have graphics that are too complex for the average printer, or color details and the average printer is black and white, these issues need to be addressed during the development phase of the change. Again, the Help Desk's involvement will help identify these types of issues.

Phase Involvement

The Help Desk's role in change management should be active and participatory. Your Help Desk should be involved in all steps relating to all system changes and their implementation.

Beginning

When the initial planning team meets to initialize the life cycle of the project, a representative from the Help Desk should be involved. This way they have input from the beginning. A change in hardware or software which may impact a group of customers in July, may not be as bad as a change impacting a group in September when there are multiple other implementations scheduled about which the programmers may not be aware. Help Desk involvement early on can help minimize the impact to customers and all support partners.

Development

The Help Desk representative should be available to the development team during the process in case their input is needed. Any meetings after the initial meeting should always include a Help Desk representative to insure they have the current status of the project and the estimated time of completion. (which can, and will, change during the life of a project)

Testing

Once the development is ready for testing, the Help Desk should be used whenever possible. If during the testing phase of the new product the Help Desk identifies issues with the product, they should have the support of the project development team to help create solutions to these problems. Whether it is hardware (adding additional RAM to 100 machines throughout the organization) or software (This screen is very confusing, and the escape key boots me out of the program), the Help Desk's input is key.

Finalization

Whenever possible, the Help Desk should have appropriate training before the product is rolled out and the related calls are received. Or if this is a small change, they need to be trained on the new aspects of the product, so they are up-to-speed before they take the first call on these issues.

A large part of change management is creating good documentation. You might make it a company policy to provide on-line documentation for the Help Desk and it's customers before the company installs new hardware or software. Not only will good documentation benefit the customers as they work their way through the new process and procedures, but it will also enable the Help Desk and its support partners provide better support to its customers.

Conclusion

As a Help Desk analyst, you act as a customer liaison to the change committee by expressing concerns regarding the impact of proposed changes from the customers' points of view. For major or new implementations, it is necessary to ensure that adequate information is available, and that there are support structures in place to provide effective problem management. Help Desks can also play a larger role in application development and design as well as systems standardization.

Practicing good change management procedures will ensure positive customer relationships during this stressful period of change.

Chapter

By Jay Boomershine

Disaster Recovery and the Help Desk

Introduction

Disaster recovery planning becomes increasingly important as businesses become more dependent on their information-processing operations. Whether your company has a full-blown contingency center or limited procedures for disaster recovery, the Help Desk usually plays a key role in facilitating communications during this critical period. Therefore, in addition to supporting the company's overall plan, Help Desk managers should create disaster recovery plans for their own centers. Your plan should be based on business cost/benefit justifications. This chapter presents tips for creating a strategic disaster recovery plan for your Help Desk.

Disaster Recovery Plan

An important document for the Help Desk is the disaster recovery plan. The purpose of a disaster recovery plan is to prepare for a catastrophe, including the loss of a data center, and rehearse a plan of action in such an instance. A study revealed that one of the safest places in the United States to build a data center is in Sante Fe, New Mexico. The rest of the country is affected by the possibility of tornados, hurricanes, earthquakes, floods, blizzards and/or volcanic eruptions. Everyone at the Help Desk needs to be aware of the disaster recovery plan for their organization, because the Help Desk normally plays a key role in facilitating communications in the event of a catastrophe.

As experienced Help Desk professionals, we are well aware of the impact of outages: i.e., how customers are affected and the length of time for recovery. Consequently, a disaster recovery plan can make or break your organization in the event of a severe natural disaster. The plan provides written documentation on which to base decisions, providing guidance for setting customer expectations should the worst-case scenario actually happen. In the unlikely event it is needed, the disaster recovery plan offers a course of action during a time of confusion and disorganization.

Common Policies

Establishing common policies across all support services groups is the first step toward a disaster recovery plan. Help Desk managers are involved in setting these policies, and Help Desk analysts need to be aware of their content and understand why they are in place. Consistency among support services groups is a starting place. For example, no matter how secure the application environment, relaxed system security will allow for manipulation of that environment. Support services' policies should set consistent levels of authorization for each department and verify that they are maintained across the organization.

Data and System Backups

Common policies are also necessary for backup and recovery of data. As a general practice, companies usually do not back up workstations. Instead, it is stressed that important work should be saved on a file server that is backed up. Should a workstation fail, this allows desk-side support to swap the customer's equipment…with minimum impact on the customer's productivity.

Fail-Safe/Redundant Configurations

Fail-safe and redundant server configurations should be part of your organization's disaster recovery plan. Servers important to daily work can be mirrored or clustered. A mirrored server allocates duplicate hardware to the same application. In a clustered server environment, the servers can have different functions but share resources across each server. In either case, if one server goes down, the other servers compensate so that the outage is transparent to the customers.

With duplicate hardware it is theoretically possible to offer true 24x7 (24 hours a day, 7 days a week) availability and to schedule outages on holidays. If one server needs maintenance, it is often possible to fix and reboot it with minimum impact on the application's availability. Customers might experience slower response times during the outage, but the application will still be available.

Remote Contingency Sites

A disaster recovery plan should address the unavailability of a location or locations. For instance, what is the corporate plan if the data center at the main offices of your corporation is no longer available? Contingency plans for running applications at a data center in a different city must be addressed in a disaster recovery plan.

There are three basic types of contingency sites: cold, warm and hot.

Cold Contingency

A cold contingency site is an alternate facility that has air-conditioning and raised flooring but no equipment installed. Servers would have to be set up and installed to duplicate the critical business functions of your organization before work could be resumed.

Warm Contingency Site

A warm contingency site has servers on site but some work would have to be done before they were operational. For example, the corporate data center could be hosted in New York and a data center for software development and testing could be located somewhere in Texas. Should one location be lost, the necessary equipment to provide service is on site at the other location, but the production applications would have to be installed before the customers could resume their work.

Hot Contingency Site

At a hot contingency site, duplicate servers will already be in place with some type of automated process that keeps them updated. If the data center was lost, the remote data center could be up and running within a couple of hours.

How to Create a Disaster Recovery Plan

Figure 12-1 presents three components Help Desk managers usually include in disaster recovery plans. These components are: [1]procedures and systems for emergency communications following a disaster, [2]emergency staffing guidelines based on the geography of the local area and home locations of key employees, and [3]emergency reconfiguration capabilities and procedures to allow partial restoration of data processing facilities.

Some plans call for companies to set up contingency operations sites with a full complement of contingency hardware and telecommunications as mentioned previously. These sites can be internal company data processing centers backing each other up, other companies' data processing centers supported by agreements to back up each other's operations, or facilities leased from companies that specialize in disaster recovery.

Some organizations establish complete disaster recovery plans, supplemented by short-term disaster recovery plans.

---

1. Procedures and systems for emergency communications following a disaster

2. Emergency staffing guidelines based on the geography of the local area and home locations of key employees

3. Emergency reconfiguration capabilities and procedures to allow partial restoration of data processing facilities

---

Figure 12-1   Three Components of a Help Desk Disaster Recovery Plan

The Help Desk plays an important role in short-term disasters such as power outages. Figure 12-2 presents four actions you'll want to include in a short-term disaster recovery plan to communicate the status of the situation to all support partners and customers. These actions could include notifying your support partners, discussing the problem, and forming anticipated outage time frames; notifying customers by using a recorded message on the incoming call message system or using other tools such as scrolling screen displays and outgoing phone calls; posting a sign in the Help Desk area to alert walk-up customers to the condition of the system; and keeping customers posted on the status of the condition and resolution.

Some organizations schedule disaster recovery drills; others periodically test portions of their disaster recovery plans. You'll need to weigh whether you should notify your staff of these drills. This is a trade-off between maximizing the spontaneous nature of the drill and minimizing the disruption it causes.

---

1. Notify all support partners, discuss the problem, and anticipate outage time frames.

2. Notify customers on the incoming call queue using a recorded message or other tools such as scrolling screen displays and outgoing phone calls.

3. Post a sign in the Help Desk area to alert walk-up customers to the condition of the system

---

Actions to include in a short-term   Figure 12-2
disaster recovery plan

Tools/Resources

To be prepared for the worse, you must have the tools and resources available to make that cross over at any time. A few of the items that you may want to develop and have available are:

• A manual trouble ticket (see Figure 12-3 for an example)

SAMPLE MANUAL TICKET

Ticket Reference Number:
Date of Call:
Time of Call:
Problem Summary:
Type of Ticket:
Severity Level:
SLA:

Caller Name:
Network Login ID:
Phone Number and Extension:
Cellphone Number:
E-Mail Address:
Department:
Location:
Computer/Workstation Name or Number:
Computer/Workstation Make & Model:
NOS & DOS:

Analyst Name:
Follow-Up Plan:

Figure 12-3   Items of information to document on a manual
trouble ticket

- A phone list of your internal and external support partners, including home address, cellphone, pager and home phone numbers.

- A phone message script list that reviews the access numbers and password to enable you to record messages on your phone system or ACD. This will allow you to quickly update the phone message greeting to let callers know of the Help Desk's current status and alternative numbers to call.

• Have an outsourced organization in place and poised for backup in case phones need to be rolled to them during any downtime for the Help Desk.

• If you support external customers, they will need to have their specific needs addressed and any special procedures to follow if your Help Desk is not available.

• Have cell phones available for your analysts to use to support special needs and to check the outsourced organizations voice message on outstanding tickets and critical needs to ensure continued support to your customers.

Publish the Help Desk Disaster Recovery Plan

Don't just make up a plan and store it away for safekeeping. Your Help Desk Web site should include information on your organization's disaster recovery policies that are currently in place and what procedures to follow. The disaster recover plans of a Help Desk should be part of your Help Desk's service-level agreement.

To simply just have a plan in place that no one knows about is a detriment to the plan itself. You must test your plan and make any necessary adjustments so it is truly ready when needed.

Disaster recovery plans are cost-effective and important to have; the development and testing of them is a cost-effective procedure.

Chapter

By Tony Bigonia

Service Level Agreements (SLA) and the Help Desk

Service level agreements (SLAs) help clarify expectations and set goals for the quality of support your Help Desk provides to its customers. Additionally, SLAs with your support partners clarifies service expectations. This chapter presents guidelines for establishing SLAs with customers as well as with external and internal support partners.

Service Level Agreements with Customers

Providing your customers with an understanding of how to best use the Help Desk and what service expectations they should have is critical in operating a successful Help Desk. Service-level agreements help you achieve these understandings. They are contracts that establish mutual expectations and provide a performance-measurement standard.

1. Help Desk hours
2. Response times associated with initial call handling
3. Average and maximum resolution times
4. Guidelines for problem resolution when various types of problems are re-assigned
5. Customer responsibilities when reporting problems
6. Help Desk procedures for keeping customers informed on the status of open problems
7. Procedures for problem escalation
8. Software products supported
9. System & Network availability
10. Data integrity, security and backup
11. Service measures to be met
12. Charge backs or cost allocations
13. Educational support
14. Monitoring & Reporting procedures
15. Signatures denoting agreement

Figure 13-1   Fifteen points to consider when drawing up SLA's with customer departments

You'll want to record in a jointly developed document any agreement between the Help Desk and one or more customer groups in your organization. This document should clearly state the level of service your Help Desk strives to provide and will help clarify customers' expectations of your Help Desk.

Figure 13-1 presents information to consider when drawing up agreements with your customers. Each SLA should be customized to meet the needs of the customer group and the business you are in. For example, if your Help Desk does not monitor system performance, then including the system availability section may not be applicable. At a minimum, these agreements should include response times, average and maximum resolution times, procedures for problem assignment and escalation, software products supported, educational support, and charge backs or cost allocations. Please note that if you commit in a service-level agreement to a resolution time for a problem, you should first understand the SLA commitments your service vendors or internal service providers are willing to guarantee before you create an agreement with the customer groups.

Service Level Management

Proper monitoring of your service is the only way to know if you are meeting your customer's expectations as spelled out in the SLA. It is critical that you think about the monitoring and reporting aspect of implementing a service-level agreement before negotiating with your customer. If you cannot prove that you are meeting the expectations that you agreed to, then the customer is open to judging the service you provide without the necessary facts. Consider waiting until you have the ability to monitor your Help Desk's performance before implementing any agreement. Because of changes in either your customer group or Help Desk, the SLA with your customer needs to be reviewed on a regular basis.

Monitoring

Whether or not you have a formal agreement, monitoring your Help Desk's service levels is important because it provides information to make ongoing improvements to better meet the needs of your customers.

Monitoring current service levels provides information on the actual level of service your Help Desk provides, tracks service improvements and provides visibility for your Help Desk. Monitoring also helps you plan staffing changes or additions, helps show achievement to motivate your staff and helps clarify your service relationship with your customers.

Service Improvement

The primary reason for monitoring service is to ensure your Help Desk is meeting its established targets as outlined in the service-level agreement. Once the Help Desk staff regularly achieves these targets, the next step is to redefine those targets and further improve levels of service.

Publishing detailed service data not only informs your staff of the services they provide, but also draws the attention of your service partners and the executive management team, which provides an opportunity for you to discuss this information with them.

Staff members providing service often feel they are working hard without achieving any concrete or positive results. Establishing targets and monitoring service performance motivates Help Desk analysts to work toward achieving and exceeding these targets and also creates a clear identity for the Help Desk.

Service Level Agreements with Support Partners

Just as service-level agreements promote understanding with your customers, such contracts with your support partners (vendors and internal service providers) provide a clear understanding of your service levels. These agreements also help you measure the quality of support your support partners provide.

Vendor Agreements

Service-level agreements with vendors can achieve a dramatic, measurable impact within your organization. Companies with established SLAs with maintenance vendors report savings of 5 to 40 percent. Some organizations justify their Help Desk budgets based on savings from such vendor SLAs.

You should expect your hardware service vendors to provide high-quality, preventive maintenance to avoid downtime. Once a problem occurs and vendors begin working toward a resolution, they should assume sufficient ownership; they should not place the problem back in the hands of the Help Desk until they have resolved the problem. This helps minimize shifting the blame or denying responsibility when the problem is not corrected in a timely manner.

Remember, to resolve a problem, vendors must go through the same cycle—and require the same time—as your Help Desk. They require time to report, dispatch, diagnose, fix and verify problem resolution.

Many vendors now offer expanded services, such as lists of known problems, on electronic bulletin boards (sometimes referred to as frequently asked questions (FAQs). Some vendors offer to become your "prime support" vendor, which means they will fix other manufacturers' products or help coordinate additional vendor services.

Monitoring Service Levels

Just as it is important for you to monitor Help Desk service levels on behalf of your customers, you need to monitor the level of support of your vendor support partners. Since agreements are often tied to dollar incentives, these measurements can have a direct financial impact on your Help Desk and can impact and clarify your Help Desk's relationship with vendors support partners.

Escalating Problems

Since contractual relationships with vendors are external, it is critical to escalate service problems promptly through the appropriate organization. In addition, the Help Desk often reports vendor responsibilities and performance to senior management. These reports help ensure your vendors actively work on timely, successful resolutions.

No other department is better positioned to capture data on vendor performance than the Help Desk. For this reason, it's important to maintain consistent and accurate records of all aspects of vendor performance.

Agreements with Internal Support Partners

Written service-level agreements with internal support partners to whom you assign problems for resolution are important, though the reason may not be obvious to your support partners. They may be concerned that an attempt to document the level of support represents unnecessary bureaucracy, or worse—a lack of trust.

From the perspective of your customers, however, these agreements are just as important as external vendor SLAs. The objective is to manage customer expectations about service delivery during a problem. If the Help Desk doesn't have established response-time service levels, then it will appear to the customer that the Help Desk analyst is not managing the problem properly.

Internal service-level agreements don't need to be lengthy or excessively detailed. The key is to include standards of performance during normal circumstances. It's also important that Help Desk management doesn't use instances where standards aren't met as clubs to beat up your support partner. Teamwork, as always, is critical.

Summary

The service-level agreement is key to your Help Desk being able to meet the customer's expectation for service. It is a negotiation between Help Desk customer management teams to determine what the Help Desk can do and what it can't do. Unrealistic expectations should not enter into the final SLA unless it is clearly defined how those expectations will be achieved. The SLA should be created either after the Help Desk has established SLAs with its support partners, or in conjunction with these groups and the customer. Include in the SLA only those areas for which the Help Desk is directly accountable, unless the necessary support groups are in involved in the development of the SLA.

Monitoring the performance of the Help Desk is key to knowing if you are meeting the targets. Remember that the SLA is a living document and will need to be reviewed on a quarterly, semiannual or annual basis due to the fluidity of business today.

Chapter 16

By John Sockrider

Measuring the Benefits of the Help Desk

What Do People Really Think of Your Help Desk?

Chapter 9 provided measurements for assessing how good your Help Desk or call center is in terms of numbers. But what do clients really think of the services you provide? How good do the people on your team think things are? To find out, all you have to do is ask. In this chapter we give you some ideas about what to ask customers and your team to determine how you're doing.

There are several approaches you should consider for getting feedback about your operation and services. You can prepare surveys to provide you with information and you can talk to people. But be prepared to act on the information you receive. In other words, don't ask questions about things that you can't or won't change. Doing so will raise expectations and when you don't deliver, will leave a poor impression on your customers and staff.

There are three information-gathering points that we will discuss here; you may have others that you like. One that we won't cover in this chapter is benchmarking your organization against competitors.

Survey Your Callers

One method of getting customer feedback is through surveys. After receiving a call, you can send out a survey to the caller, asking for feedback on how well his/her call was handled. Consider taking a random sample of incoming calls or use every 50th or 100th call and send a survey to the caller. You can send out the survey using a manual process; however, your call-tracking system may have the capability to do this. Keep your survey sample small enough so that you aren't inundated with replies, but large enough to give you a good representation.

If the call-tracking system can't do the survey, you may still be able to automate it with a small amount of programming. Use your reporting tools to extract a sample of the calls from your database. Send an e-mail to the selected client with the survey questions that they can complete and return to you. You may also be able to point them to the survey that is on your intranet. Any of these methods would allow you to have different questions for different types of calls.

There are also survey providers on the Internet that will post the survey and compile the results for you.

Use the results of the survey to make improvements where appropriate, but also use them to publicize how well your Help Desk is doing. If you have gathered cost figures for support in your organization, you can tie costs into the survey results and show how the Help Desk is reducing costs by minimizing the occurrence of problems or by resolving problems in a timely manner. In addition, the Help Desk may be freeing other technicians to work on planning and regular maintenance instead of problem resolution.

There are several reasons to do surveys:

1. To monitor performance according to stated service level commitments.
2. To monitor your client's perception of your service.
3. To obtain ideas for improvement.
4. To identify trends.
5. To improve clients' perceptions of the help desk by demonstrating an interest in clients' opinions.

In drafting questions for the survey, keep in mind what your vision, mission, goals, and values are. Ask questions the answers to which will provide ideas that will let you improve in ways that are consistent with your vision, mission, goals, and values. Unless you are trying to build a case for some major changes, you may not want to ask about things that you cannot change. Let's take a look at some sample questions that you can ask each of these groups.

SAMPLE SURVEY FOR CLIENTS WHO RECENTLY CALLED YOUR CENTER

1. How long did you have to remain on the line before a Help Desk analyst answered your call?
   - ☐ Not too long.
   - ☐ Too long.

2. If the Help Desk analyst was able to resolve your problem while you were on the phone with him/her, how long did it take to resolve your problem?
   - ☐ Not too long.
   - ☐ Too long.

3. If the analyst was able to provide you with a solution to your problem while you were on the phone, did this completely resolve your concerns?
   - ☐ Yes
   - ☐ No

4. If the answer to question 3 was no, please explain.

5. If the Help Desk analyst had to reassign your ticket to someone else to work on your request, did the analyst tell you when you could expect a call back regarding the ticket?
   - ☐ Yes
   - ☐ No

6. If your problem was not resolved during the initial call, did you receive a call back within the time frame that you were quoted?
   - ☐ Yes
   - ☐ No

7. (Some call tracking systems can send a copy of the ticket to the client via email. If your system does that, ask the following question.) Was the description of your problem accurate?
   - ☐ Yes
   - ☐ No

8. Did someone keep you informed of the status of your ticket through-out the duration of your problem?
   - ☐ Yes
   - ☐ No

9. If your ticket was assigned to an analyst outside of the Help Desk, did that analyst resolve the problem to your satisfaction?
   - ☐ Yes
   - ☐ No

10. Was your problem resolved in a timely manner?
    - ☐ Yes
    - ☐ No

11. What is your perception of the level of service provided to you on this problem?
    - ☐ Poor
    - ☐ Adequate
    - ☐ Excellent

12. If you have any suggestions or criticisms for the Help Desk, please use the space below to express your thoughts and opinions.

Always ask for and leave room for written comments.

Interview Your Most Frequent Users

Another resource for information is periodically contacting your most frequent callers or representatives of departments or client organizations that you serve. You can do this with a survey once or twice a year. However, there is value in conducting a phone interview or a face-to-face meeting with them. Not only does it give more candid information, but also it fosters great public relations.

The best person to talk to is probably a "power user" of the technology that you support. That person may be the "expert" in his or her department to whom other people go with questions. Therefore, he/she will have insight into the department's needs. They may regard you as representing not only the Help Desk, but also all of your support partners. So you should be prepared to gather information that you can use for the Help Desk and that you can pass on to your support partners.

You will want to discuss the interactions they've had with your organization, both good and bad. Get specific examples if you can. Also discuss their needs and whether they are being met. This is a great opportunity to get their view of what they will be doing in their department in the future that might impact your Help Desk.

Have Your Team Do Their Own Evaluation

A third source of information is letting your team members evaluate their performance and offer suggestions for improvement. They will have the most, and perhaps the best, ideas about how to improve your operation and performance.

Use the following items to have your team members evaluate how well the team is working together. Have each team member evaluate how the team is doing and then discuss as a group how to improve the team's operation.

Team Goals: Are there clear and specific goals for the team? When goals are developed, is it done through a group process of team interaction and agreement? Is each team member willing to work toward achieving these goals?

Participation: Do all team members participate actively and are the tasks and roles of the team shared? Is there a feeling of group togetherness?

Feedback: Do the team members ask for feedback? Do team members use feedback to help each other out? Is feedback used to clarify the feelings and interests of the team members?

Team Decision Making: Does the team have a process that encourages active participation by all members?

Leadership: Is leadership distributed and shared among team members? Do individuals willingly contribute their resources as needed?

Problem Solving: Do all team members encourage discussion of team issues? Do all team members participate in critiquing team effectiveness?

Conflict: Conflict should not be suppressed. Dealing with and managing conflict should be seen as a way to improve team performance.

Team Member Resources: Are the abilities and talents of the team members recognized and utilized as well as they should be?

Risk Taking and Creativity: Is reasonable risk taking encouraged? Are mistakes viewed as an opportunity for learning?

Use Survey Results to Improve

After reviewing the results of any of these feedback methods, the Help Desk team should determine the areas they want to improve and establish a strategy for doing so. After you make changes, follow up with your clients to see if your changes have made a noticeable impact.

Chapter

By Donna Holt

Help Desk Certification

Why Certify?

We've been certifying products and services for decades. The Good Housekeeping Seal of Approval has been around as long as most of us can remember. Product guarantees and quality programs are all around us. They lend credibility to products and services, much the same way accredited learning institutions award diplomas for completing a course of study.

Webster defines the word certify as, "to declare (a thing) true, accurate, etc., by formal statement." A certificate is, "a document attesting to a fact, qualification, etc." Certification in the help desk industry is a measurement of the performance of an individual or organization.

Help Desk Certification Programs

There have been accreditations for computer technology specialists for many years. However, it has only been in the past few years that the industry began recognizing those of us at the help desk as professionals. The growth of the help desk industry has sparked the desire for programs that bring certification and professionalism to this industry.

Surfing the Web will produce many more hits on the word, "certification" than on the words, "Help Desk Certification". However, there are now several organizations offering help desk certification. Help Desk Institute has the only standards based certification guided by open industry committees.

Certification of Support Organizations

HDI's Site Certification program is based on 60 internationally recognized standards and focuses on eight core areas required for providing a state-of-the-art support operation.

HDI's Site Certification program was developed by an open industry standards committee for the support industry. Help Desk Institute took a leading role in forming the HDI Open Standards and Site Certification Committee. This initiative is an international effort with participants from the United States, Canada, Europe and Japan working jointly to define the criteria and methodology for support-center evaluation. The committee is dedicated to creating an industry wide blueprint for support centers to follow. Committee members include representatives from a wide variety of leading organizations including:

- Bank of America – USA
- Japan Help Desk Center – Japan
- North Highlands – USA
- Service Management International – USA
- Sun Microsystems – USA
- CSM Europe – UK
- NCR Corporation – USA
- PinkRecords – Canada
- Sprint – USA
- W.H.S. Consulting Group Ltd – Germany

The committee specializes in developing the open standards for individual industry professionals and help desk centers, and is dedicated to the continual improvement of these industry-wide blueprints.

HDI's certification committee believes that the journey toward certification is as important as the certification itself. HDI provides the open standards and site certification output as a road map to certification giving any organization access to the committee's continually improving definition of quality.

Not every support center will achieve certification status, but all that follow the path will be better for the effort.

The benefits of achieving certified support center status are numerous and include:

- Heightened credibility
- Increased profitability
- Improved employee morale
- Measurement tools that provide benchmarks for organizational growth
- Maintenance of industry performance standards

But, more importantly, the process provides the necessary information needed to strategically plan for future success. The program enables organizations to accurately measure their compliance with current best practice and recognized standards.

HDI has a number of tools available to assist you in preparing for the site certification audit.

Site Certification Standards	Open standards available on the HDI Web site.
Certified Auditors	HDI's Certified Auditors possess skills necessary to perform accurate and professional audits within the HDI site certification program. They can also assist you to prepare for audit (by another independent certified auditor) through their consultancy services.
Online Self Evaluation	This very valuable tool is available to HDI members only. It is an interactive questionnaire that provides valuable audit information and insight into your site's readiness for certification. Once complete, the self evaluation program generates a report to show how your site compares to the standards.
Site Certification Training Course	This course is a must if you intend to become an HDI Certified Auditor, an internal auditor or if you are preparing for certification and want to know, first hand, what auditors will be looking for.

Certification of Individuals

How is HDI Certification different from other Help Desk certification programs?

HDI's individual certification program is based on internationally recognized, open standards designed by IT Help Desk experts, consultants, industry leaders and practitioners. The first of its kind to be launched in the industry, the program creates a set of practices and a recognized career path for the Help Desk and IT support industry worldwide. The aim? To improve Help Desk standards and to establish a structured education and career path for the industry.

The benefits of becoming certified are numerous and include:

• Professional recognition by peers and employers
• A sense of professional accomplishment
• Professional advancement and promotion
• New employment opportunities

People who earn their certification through HDI's programs have met the requirements necessary for a help desk professional (as identified by the standards committee), have been acknowledged by the industry's most respected organization for their excellence and can be assured that their certification will be recognized worldwide.

Help Desk Institute's certification programs are not based on subjective training programs. They are based on standards set by the industry for the industry.

HDI's Individual Certification program has four levels universally reflecting the key job functions in the IT support and Help Desk industry.

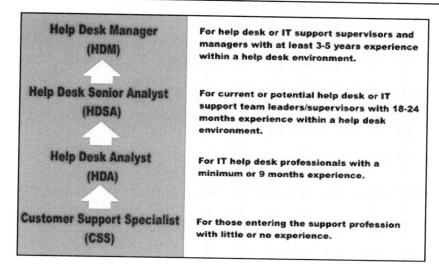

Help Desk Manager (HDM)	For help desk or IT support supervisors and managers with at least 3-5 years experience within a help desk environment.
Help Desk Senior Analyst (HDSA)	For current or potential help desk or IT support team leaders/supervisors with 18-24 months experience within a help desk environment.
Help Desk Analyst (HDA)	For IT help desk professionals with a minimum or 9 months experience.
Customer Support Specialist (CSS)	For those entering the support profession with little or no experience.

Certified Customer Support Specialist

A Certified Customer Support Specialist (entry level position) will:

- Gain knowledge and understanding about the expectations of the role and the customer service environment
- Learn the importance of the role from customer and business perspectives
- Understand the importance of and techniques to maintain customer loyalty
- Understand the importance of using best practices in the customer service environment

Certified Help Desk Analyst

The Help Desk Analyst (HDA) certification is for IT Help Desk professionals with at least 9 months experience of working in the IT Help Desk environment.

A Certified Help Desk analyst will:

- Understand the role of the Help Desk analyst
- Be equipped with the tools and techniques needed to excel as an analyst
- Work within internationally recognized guidelines and standards
- Be committed to customer service excellence

Certified Help Desk Senior Analyst

The Help Desk Senior Analyst (HDSA) certification is for experienced IT support analysts, project managers and Help Desk support consultants with at least 18-24 months experience of working in the IT Help Desk environment. It is specifically designed for those who manage process re-engineering and service delivery and individuals responsible for selecting, purchasing, implementing and maintaining support tools and technologies.

A Certified Help Desk Senior Analyst will:
- Understand the technologies, processes and key factors to consider in order to optimize Help Desk performance
- Design a new support center, or analyze an existing center
- Consult on performance enhancements
- Re-engineer a support center

Certified Help Desk Manager

The Help Desk Manager (HDM) certification is for experienced IT Help Desk supervisors, managers and projects managers with at least 3-5 years experience in the IT Help Desk support industry. It is specifically for managers who are responsible for the day-to-day operation of the IT Help Desk.

A Certified Help Desk Manager will:
- Manage service levels with customers and secondary support personnel
- Conduct team building exercises
- Exhibit excellent financial skills
- Conduct change and asset management
- Perform staff scheduling and work-force planning
- Measure customer satisfaction
- Determine appropriate use of technology

Certification Exams

To ensure the security of the tests and the results, HDI Certification tests are proctered exams. This is considered a must for quality of results. HDI exams may be taken at Prometric, a Thomson Learning Company or VUE, an NCS Person Business, both available at thousands of locations around the world. Specific information can be obtained on the HDI Web site.

Recognized Training Providers (RTP) support the HDI open standards and are committed to creating a career structure for Help Desk professionals.

RTP's are established training organizations the currently provide their own courses for Help Desk professionals. Their courseware has been methodically 'mapped and tracked' against HDI open standards and is recognized and endorsed by HDI.

To find out more about becoming a Recognized Training Provider and having your courseware mapped and tracked against HDI individual certification standards please contact the HDI certification team.